brilliantideas

one good idea can change your life...

Smarter business start-ups

Start your dream business

Jon Smith

First published in 2005 by
The Infinite Ideas Company Limited
Belsyre Court
57 Woodstock Road
Oxford
OX2 6HJ
United Kingdom
www.infideas.com

A CIP catalogue record for this book is available from the British Library.

ISBN 1-904902-26-X

Designed and typeset by Baseline Arts Ltd, Oxford
Printed and bound by TJ International, Cornwall

Brilliant ideas

Brilliant features

Each chapter of this book is designed to provide you with an inspirational idea that you can read quickly and put into practice straight away.

Throughout you'll find four features that will help you to get right to the heart of the idea:

- *Try another idea* If this idea looks like a life-changer then there's no time to lose. *Try another idea* will point you straight to a related tip to expand and enhance the first.
- *Here's an idea for you* Give it a go – right here, right now – and get an idea of how well you're doing so far.
- *Defining ideas* Words of wisdom from masters and mistresses of the art, plus some interesting hangers-on.
- *How did it go?* If at first you do succeed try to hide your amazement. If, on the other hand, you don't this is where you'll find a Q and A that highlights common problems and how to get over them.

Introduction

It's the middle of the night, or during a particularly long session in a public house and Eureka – there you have it. An idea that is just so brilliant, onlookers are going to need sunglasses. You will be richer than you could have possibly imagined and the world will be a much better place, all because of you.

So you mention the idea to one or two others, and more than likely they are nodding in agreement. It doesn't get any easier than this, until, the first blow – a question – innocuous enough, but you're not able to answer. Your idea hasn't necessarily got holes (not yet anyway), it just needs to be thought through that bit more. It's time to plan the business properly. Starting a business is possibly one of the most exciting, exhilarating and rewarding experiences available to mankind (except perhaps winning £15 million on the national lottery). But it's not easy. Starting a business comes with a huge risk to your finances, your friendships and possibly even your health. More and more start-ups are not surviving beyond the first twelve months of operations, and for some the failure of the business leads to bankruptcy. So, with all of the odds apparently stacked against you, should your idea remain just that?

No. New businesses can be incredibly successful. Like anything, you have to use the tricks of the trade and ensure your idea stands the greatest chance of success.

Smarter business start-ups will show you how to plan effectively to create the business you want, help kick your competition into touch and have bank managers falling over themselves to let you borrow money...Well, maybe not the latter, but still, not bad for thirteen quid!

The key to a successful business is clear and simple planning from the outset. So why is there any need to read on? Well, paradoxically keeping things clear and simple is actually quite difficult and fraught with problems.

So how can these difficulties and problems be overcome by reading just one book? Simple – by addressing the target audience directly, in an organised and logical way and in the language suitable for the task in hand. In a word, clear – tailored for the entrepreneur, requiring only as many words as are needed to address the points, and no more.

So why are there no direct examples from the annals of time showing how a simple idea became a multi-national success? Well, unless you are the same company, selling exactly the same products or services at the same time, someone else's planning won't work for you. Each of the 52 brilliant ideas contained in this book will matter to you, in different ways and to different degrees. You have an idea for a business in today's market and they had theirs. Your opportunities will differ and you may or may not be targeting the same consumer base.

Everyone has an idea for a business at some stage in their life – for many it is a pipe dream, but for a brave few it is the seed of a plan that they take to fruition. Starting a business and making it a success is all about knowing what you need to do to give yourself the strongest chance of surviving, and profiting, in an already saturated market. We all have our own ideas about how things should work, how things should run and how much things should cost, and no matter what your business idea may be, there are still processes that must be followed, documents that need writing and research to be undertaken before your business can be launched. Before embarking on any of the chapters contained in this book, can you answer these questions? Who is your target market? Where are they? How much will they spend on your products or service? How strong is your competition? Can you raise the finance required? And, most importantly, how will the public and consumers react to your business? How can consumers find you? Has this been done before, and failed? Why do you want or need to start a business? *Smarter business start-ups* assumes no previous experience; it is for you, the entrepreneur, to empower *you* to talk to the people you need to involve on this adventure about *what you want* and more importantly, *what you do not want*.

So how do you use this book? Dip in and dip out, read it from start to finish – It really doesn't matter. The 52 brilliant ideas contained within are proven tips that should result in immediate benefits to you and your business, if adopted. If your budget is modest, implementing just a handful of ideas *will* improve your idea and *will* help you realise your ambitions and the ambitions of your business. Employ all 52 and you should be looking at a very comfortable retirement in the next eighteen months – no wait, I mean you should be in a much stronger position to take your business idea forward and turn your dreams into reality.

1

Playing the name game

Deciding upon a name for a business is like naming a child. This business is your progeny and you'll want to help it grow and mature over the coming years.

Naming the business can mean hours of agonising before finally making a decision. Do have fun when choosing a name for your business, but make sure you can tell it to your friends without giggling.

Why all the fuss? Having a badly chosen name for a company will not do you any favours when promoting your business. A name that is difficult for the public (or worse, for staff members) to pronounce is a little embarrassing, if you are forever correcting them. A name that conjures images of a completely different product or service will simply cause confusion. Unless the name of the business came to you in a prophetic dream along with the completed business plan, then this is a decision that should be taken carefully and involve as many people as you can. Remember, your friends and family are also consumers and will be very honest about what they think about your potential names.

Here's an idea for you...

Draw up a shortlist of ten names for your business. Now get as many other people as you can to put your list into their preferred order. Is there an overall favourite? You should see a pattern forming and if your pollsters are willing to expand on the rationale for their choice, you might better understand why your own choice is great or even a potential disaster. Remember, names are incredibly subjective and you the business owner do and should have the final say on what name to go for – but do listen to your potential customers and clients.

During the decision-making process be sure to search for any names that you are considering on your national register (in the UK, you can do this at the Companies House website) to ascertain whether any other company has or is trading with that name already. Note that you *can* trade under a name that has been used in the past as long as that company is now dissolved. If this is a route you wish to pursue, and no other name will do, try to find out as much as you can about the dissolved company – the last thing you want to do is to bring any bad will or negative press associated with that company to your own. This is particularly important if you are operating a very similar business or intending to sell the same products or services. For example, it wouldn't be a particularly shrewd move to launch an online

clothes retailer called Boo.com following the highly publicized collapse of a dotcom clothes retailer of that name.

Something clicks into place at the very moment that you decide upon a name for your business. Whether it turns out to be hours, days or months of deliberation, when the judges' result is revealed your business will have a home. Now you are able to refer to your business on first name terms rather than just saying 'we're going to sell such and such in a chain of shops around the country'. This immediately helps towards creating a brand and brand awareness. Every time you talk about the business to others, you will be reinforcing the name, and they, in turn, will tell others.

Try another idea...

Naming a business is the first step to creating a brand. To learn more about branding, check out IDEA 2, *Big, bold and a little bit cheeky*.

Defining idea...

'Condense some daily experience into a glowing symbol, and an audience is electrified.'

RALPH WALDO EMERSON

Defining idea...

'We do what we must, and call it by the best names.'

RALPH WALDO EMERSON

How did it go?

Q The other directors want to use a classical reference as our company name. It is deliberately obscure, but the knock-on effect is that everyone we ask for an opinion replies 'what does that mean?' Will it work?

A An obscure name is not necessarily a bad one, especially if it is memorable. I doubt that many people know that 'Nike' means 'victory' in Greek, but look at how powerful that name and business has become. A good name becomes *the business and even a brand in its own right. If you like the name, go with it. Another sportswear company, Adidas, got its name from its German founder, Adi Dassler.*

Q We have reduced ten possible names down to two, but can't decide which is better. Each seems equally appealing and sums up our business idea perfectly. What can we do to tip the balance?

A It can happen that several potential names all seem perfect for the job. You are going to have to pick one of them, though – if placing the names into a hat and picking one out doesn't seem quite professional enough, do some more research and produce a mock-up of a logo and brand design for each name. Seeing the brands visually will quickly decide your overall winner. Big companies often interview 'focus groups' of consumers to get more insight into how brands and names are perceived. You could try this inexpensively with a group of friends.

2

Big, bold and a little bit cheeky

Creating a logo and a name for a business are closely connected and should really be decided upon at the same time. Remember, your business name and logo will become your brand.

In today's image-conscious world, branding has never been more important. If you are able to tap into the Zeitgeist, you will be well on your way to success.

One important tip: avoid at all costs a logo that looks in any way like male genitals – this is surprisingly easy to do by accident, and it won't win you many customers!

There's always a rush associated with launching a new business, often because there has already been a financial outlay and you need to get to market as soon as possible to recoup, or because you fear that someone else might be about to launch a similar business. Either way, you simply cannot rush the creation of your logo.

Here's an idea for you...

Walk down any high street and take note of ten household brands. What style have they chosen for their logos? What image does the logo project? Your business may never need to appear on the high street, but imagine if your brand is eventually just as powerful and recognisable to the casual onlooker.

Do not be tempted to use one of the pre-designed (copyright-free) logos you can find in computer design software. Even if it is only supposed to be a temporary measure, people who see this logo may recognise it as not your own creation; even if they don't, they will probably think that it looks a little tacky.

Don't forget, the people you will be meeting during the creation of your business will be people or companies that you are hoping to have a long-term relationship with, such as your suppliers, customers, solicitors, accountants, investors and the bank. Of all the people that you will be dealing with, these should be the most important in terms of creating the right impression. Don't sell yourself short so early on. Pay the fee and have a designer create your logo; they may not be particularly cheap, but good designers are worth their weight in gold.

DON'T BE SHY

When considering a design or briefing a designer it is important not to insist on too many boundaries. Although you might have a very clear idea about how the brand should look and even the colours or fonts to be used, make it clear that you would like to see any other ideas the designer might have. The results will be strange, exciting, worrying and sometimes amusing, but what this exercise shows is how brands elicit powerful reactions in people. Use focus groups and informal market surveys to see

Defining idea...

'Do not, for one repulse, forego the purpose that you resolved to effect.'
WILLIAM SHAKESPEARE

how people feel about your logo. The more people you can find to comment on the designs for your logo, the better. It will quickly become apparent which one will work best to project the image that you want.

Try another idea...

Your logo will be the first of many branding decisions that you will take. To find out more, check out IDEA 9, *Just needs a lick of paint.*

FLIRTING WITH MEDIA

Another consideration when designing your logo should be whether it is suitable for all media. Although you may not intend to launch a website for your business, you should still find out how your logo would look at the top of a webpage. Would the logo work on a TV screen or on an enormous advertising hoarding in a big city? If your staff are going to wear uniforms, or if you plan to issue company T-shirts, is the logo transferable onto clothing? Does the logo work for you when it is very large, or very small? Ask your designer to work with a range of colours and also to create a version using only black and one other colour. Sometimes simple colours work best and if you use a whole rainbow of colours in your logo it will cost a lot more to reproduce. Full colour letterheads, business cards and adverts are considerably more expensive than two-colour versions. But don't lose sight of the main goal – you are creating a brand that you want to be stunning, instantly recognisable and with the potential to become synonymous with your business. If it costs a little extra to create the sign above the door because you simply have to have aquamarine blue, so be it.

Defining idea...

'There is nothing worse than a sharp image of a fuzzy concept.'
ANSEL ADAMS

How did it go?

Q High street shops are consumer-facing but our business is going to be b2b (business to business) and the values we need to project are completely different. Surely we shouldn't look at consumer goods brands for ideas?

A *Whether your customers are members of the public or businesses, they still want to see the same thing: a logo that is well thought out and projects expertise, knowledge and value for money. You need to make your customers feel that your firm is a company that can be trusted. There is nothing worse than a poorly designed logo that makes you look like a cowboy – except, perhaps, for one that makes you look as if your offerings will be grossly overpriced! Your brand and logo should reflect the market opportunity you have identified; if you are competing on price, say, or you are offering a high-quality bespoke service, this should be implied by the designs you create.*

Q My partners and I can't seem to agree on the designs and I'm trying to whittle them down to a choice of two or three. Are there any things that should definitely be avoided?

A *It is not good practice to have a logo that looks similar to one that already exists. It won't fool consumers and makes you look a bit dishonest, especially if the other company is a global success. In the cut-throat world of food retailing, there are occasionally attempts to mimic a brand or package design in the hope that customers will buy a product by accident, thinking it is a more famous brand. Major lawsuits usually follow.*

3

Beg, borrow and steal

If you are looking for capital from outside sources, it's not enough to show you are passionate about the idea – you must have a business plan and the prospect of a good return for your investors.

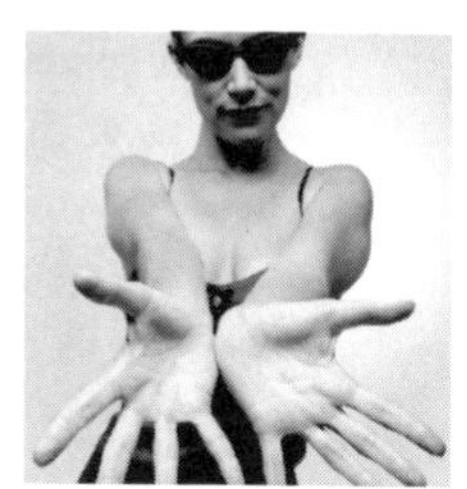

You do lose some control by inviting others in to finance your business, but often there would be no business without their help; investors may bring useful skills along with their money.

Investment capital will make or break your business. Get your hands on as much of it as you possibly can, even if it means telling a few white lies.

When you have a great idea for a business, it is often quite difficult to understand why everyone is very happy to talk to you about it until you mention that it needs some funding. Suddenly there is an awkward silence and people make their excuses and leave.

The best possible scenario is that you are launching the business with your own capital that you have just lying around in a deposit account, but the chances of this are very slim. You may have to sell assets to raise cash, or you may have to borrow or seek outside investors.

Here's an idea for you...

Take time to set up the right bank account for your business. A common mistake is simply to go with your personal bankers. Personal and business accounts work very differently and are run by different staff – so your twenty years of loyalty may not be rewarded. Choose the bank that the offers best product for the lowest cost.

It is important to exhaust your own means of raising cash before asking for any more from anyone else. Every penny counts because the more you borrow from others the more you will have to pay back, and the more control over your business you will lose. If you can reduce that amount by even a small sum, it will help.

Do not sell yourself short and pretend that if you sell the car to raise money, you can always buy another one once the company gets started. This won't happen and you will be without a car for a long, long time. Only sell assets that you can really do without. Look to raise money by selling off unused items you own, such as old CDs, DVDs or furniture. Many of us own a lot of extra stuff that we do not use that is sitting in boxes in our own or, even worse, other people's houses. Make these items work for you and sell them. There are the traditional routes such as car-boot and garage sales, but with the glut of online auction houses and Amazon's marketplace program, you can start selling very easily.

No matter how generous your friends and family are, they will all think very hard and long before deciding to become involved. It really isn't distrust of your ability to set up a business and make it happen, or revenge for all the times you left your friends to pay the bar bill. There is something inherent within us all that makes us wary of investing in start-ups. The statistics back this up; a staggering number of start-up ventures fail.

If they are happy to invest, you must provide them with the same information that a professional lender such as a bank would require: a business plan and some financial projections. In your own mind, treat them as a lender and set up a realistic payment plan through direct debit, so both parties know how the relationship will work out. Again, if your lender is looking to recoup their capital and receive a return on profits, it is in everyone's interests if a solicitor formulates this relationship professionally – a gentleman's agreement really isn't enough if things go a bit sour.

Try another idea...

When accepting funding from an investor, you are probably going to have to relinquish some control of the business. To learn more, check out IDEA 26, *Selling out before you have begun.*

BANKING ON IT

Banks are a safe way to borrow money. Although their interest rates are very high, everyone knows where they stand. The bank will insist on forms being signed and, if the loan is taken out by the company, they will ask for some security (depending on the amount), which could be your home or other assets. They may also require that the directors agree to take on loan repayments should the company fail. By going through a bank, you will be asked to provide the all-important business plan and financial statements which will have been completed prior to the money being paid over – so at least you will have a clear plan that you can start implementing the moment the cash comes through.

Defining idea...

'Drive-in banks were established so most of the cars today could see their real owners.'

E. JOSEPH CROSSMAN, poet

How did it go?

Q I have looked at four different banks and all of their charges are astronomical. Which one should I choose?

A *It is a shock to the system to see how much it costs just to present a cheque or phone your bank with a query. The secret is to look at what charges you are likely to incur in your first year. For new businesses, I would suggest looking at the banks that offer the best overdraft facilities.*

Q Do I really need internet banking?

A *You can live without it, but you will find that managing your finances and viewing your balance online is a huge benefit to your business. Start the process of applying for an online registration immediately as it can take weeks, if not months, to complete.*

Q A friend tells me that it is better in the long run to borrow than to give shares of a business to investors? Is this true?

A. *This is a hot topic in corporate finance, and even major firms consider all their options when starting a new venture. For us lesser mortals, it is a trade-off between the high cost of borrowing, which can kill a business, and giving away too great a share of something that might become very valuable. That's why using your own money is the best solution of all; it's cheaper than borrowing and you retain control.*

4

Who wants some?

For the business to work you need customers. Do you know who your customers will be? Are you sure you know? What proof do you have?

Many people start a business because they are looking for a lifestyle change and a chance to do a job properly. The best reason, though, is because you feel it will be profitable.

Customers are a bit scary and some of them may not be people you would like to meet in a dark alley, but you need to explore their needs and behaviour. It is important to decide on your stereotypical customer, both in your own mind and for the purposes of defining your consumers within your business plan. What you write will not be set in stone – there will always be consumers buying your products that you would never have imagined (octogenarians buying sportswear to run a marathon, for instance) – but the vast majority of your customers will fall in to a standardized category. Once this has been defined you will be in a better position to know exactly what it is you are researching and, once the business has launched, how best to market yourself and your products to that group.

Here's an idea for you...

Identify your target customer. If you can define it precisely as, say, a 16- to 32-year-old cash-rich male, you are on the right track. You will not be painting yourself into a corner or alienating investors or consumers by acknowledging this.

The internet can provide you with a vast amount of information, ranging from the entirely useless to the highly informative, to help you in your quest to start a business. Use the internet tirelessly to uncover stats and numbers for a better understanding of who is currently buying the products or services that you are considering providing and who is likely to want to consume if you were to let them know about your existence. Start with government sites and consumer groups that can provide you with demographics, average spend, trends and patterns found in the area of business that you are planning to enter.

Whether you are looking to borrow from the bank, or from other sources, you will require a bank account and therefore you will be booked in for a meeting with a business manager. During this meeting give as much information as you can about your business and your target audience. Many banks provide fact sheets on starting specific businesses (especially in certain areas of retail and catering) if you ask, which can sometimes be useful.

Defining idea...

'Basic research is what I am doing when I don't know what I am doing.'

WERNHER VON BRAUN

There are top-level research reports you can buy (they tend to be expensive) that will provide you with huge amounts of data and information about specific products, industries or consumer trends. It is well worth investigating what organisations such as Mintel hold on the area you would like to investigate – their reports are costly but they take a lot of the hard work out of research.

Try another idea...

Understanding your potential customers will also help you plan the potential revenues and take-up you can expect once your business is launched. To learn more, check out IDEA 6, *Cheap at twice the price*.

If you don't have much business experience, you may be overoptimistic about how many customers you can acquire. Remember that demand is what drives sales. In some businesses, such as being a landlord, it is quite easy to assess the demand for your offering by studying rental property in a certain area. In others, such as marketing consumer products, it is much more difficult to know whether any customers will buy, especially if you hope to sell through major distribution channels that may not have your best interests at heart. Make sure that you have really good evidence that people will buy before you launch the business. One way to do this is to try small-scale pilot schemes; one small business I know tried several different ways of marketing their products on a small scale and discovered that only one method was profitable. This kind of information could save you a fortune if you discover it early on.

Defining idea...

'Research is the process of going up alleys to see if they are blind.'

MARSTON BATES, American author

How did it go?

Q Our business is quite specific and we can't find much evidence of any research having been conducted. We feel we're a pretty unique offering, and we'll have to go into it blind. Are we right to think along these lines?

A *No business is truly unique. Your plan may have unique aspects to it, but fundamentally all businesses are selling products or services, no matter how 'fresh' your take might be. Even if the product is brand-new on the market and you are the sole seller, there are still things to be learned from related products, or the product's predecessor. Never launch a business blind.*

Q We are planning to launch a coffee shop located near to a busy train station. Our customer base is obvious and it will be a resounding success. Research is to simply stand at the entrance of the train station and see the throng of people every day. How can it fail?

A *Although it might appear to be a foregone conclusion that your business idea will work in the location you have chosen, are there any properties available exactly where you need them? How about the competition? The fact that hundreds, even thousands, of people pass your business every day does not guarantee sales. You still need to research who buys your product or service and work out how many of them are walking past.*

5

What's in your pocket?

You will need to determine how many customers you can expect per day, month and year and how much each of them will spend on your products and services.

Although nobody is expecting absolute accuracy, very few people will be fooled by sheer hope. Picking numbers out of the sky is one sure way to complete your projections quickly – but the document will be useless.

Dust off the calculator and prepare yourself for the joy of profit and loss sheets! In some respects you *can* get away with producing any old figures to present in your business plan – but the only person that you will be deceiving is yourself. No one can project figures completely accurately, but it is better to take an educated guess, based on the hard facts and the research that you have conducted, than to just make them up.

Here's an idea for you...

If you have three routes to market, say high street retail sales, internet sales and mail order, revise the figures so that your original focus becomes secondary and you are now dependent on one of the other routes (say, mail order instead of high street retail). How does this alter your sales projections and customer spend?

A huge mistake is to view both the creation of the business plan and the financial statements as a chore that you need to complete for someone else's benefit. Primarily they are both documents that you need to create for yourself and revise religiously; other people will need to see them along the way, but the primary audience is you. The best business plans are referred to again and again. These documents should become the benchmark by which you judge yourself, not abandoned files that are demoted to the third drawer of your filing cabinet. They will act as anchors to stop you vying off on a particular tangent and they will be a great indicator as to whether things are going as well as they should be.

If it turns out, very quickly, that the figures you have projected have become either unachievable or desperately under actual performance, then you can alter your future projections accordingly. Get out of the mindset that your projected sales are merely figures you need to create in order to secure finance and get the project off to a start. They are *your* future and the more accurately you can predict future success, the more chance you have of securing the finance that you require in the first place; and making your business a resounding success.

If the data exist, then you will quickly be able to determine the size of the market from websites and paid-for research. Next, decide how much of the market you intend to command after one, two and three years of operations. If you know the value of the entire market, you can work out the value of your projected market share.

Try another idea...

It's very easy, when planning a business, to work out how much you are going to earn, but equally important in the numbers game is to work out how much you are going to spend gaining that business. To learn more about budgeting for expenditure, check out IDEA 6, *Cheap at twice the price.*

When creating your financial spreadsheet you can break that figure down into the number of customers required and the average customer spend. It's not exact, but you have a starting figure that indicates how much you feel is achievable; this is the number of customers expected to buy from you, and how much they will be spending.

Now consider the factors that could affect your plans: the time it will take you to get up to speed; what if the competition raises their game? What if there is a sudden depression in the market? How would it affect your particular line of business, if interest rates suddenly sky-rocketed and consumer confidence was shattered? Would you be the first or last industry to feel the pinch? These are valid questions that you must consider, not ignore. Notice that you have moved forward, away from guessing wildly just to make the business plan visually exciting and attractive.

Defining idea...

'All progress is based upon a universal innate desire on the part of every organism to live beyond its income.'
SAMUEL BUTLER, 19th century author and critic

How did it go?

Q Our business relies upon client meetings, which simply cannot be replicated on the net or mail order – we really only have one sales channel. Why should we invest in the web and advertising at all?

A *Although closing the deal may rely upon a face-to-face meeting, there are still valuable marketing and promotion opportunities to be had via the net and mail order. Instead of looking at these as direct routes to the actual sale, see them as promotional activities. What if you, or an outside source, were to promote your offerings in different ways and earn you contacts – is there a commission structure you could devise, in payment for their efforts, and would the extra business they bring add to your bottom line? At the very least, you can use your website as an updatable product catalogue that existing and potential clients can access.*

Q With our low staffing levels we would be too stretched to launch three sales channels effectively. What should we look at first, mail order or a website?

A *Look at the internet first, mainly because it will cost a lot less to get a functioning site operational, the information can be altered far more easily and you can keep building extra pages when resources allow it.*

6

Cheap at twice the price

If you spend more than you have before the business is even launched, you're setting yourself up for disaster.

If you overestimate how much revenue you expect to make in your first year then there are still a few options open to you that will mean the books balance at the end of twelve months.

The most successful businesses are those than plan expenditure right down to the last penny, and stick to it. Sticking to a budget is as hard as sticking to a diet – but to run a fit and healthy business you need to avoid eating all the pies before breakfast is served. You will grossly underestimate how much even the basic things cost to buy – coupled with the desire, every now and again, to break the budget on one or two items that you just must have to make your business a resounding success. Then there are the items that you accidentally hadn't budgeted for and come in as emergency purchases the weeks, or days, before launch. Added together, you are likely to go 5–20% over budget – and that's *with* sound planning!

Here's an idea for you...

Look to save on the ancillary costs of running your premises. Just saving half a per cent on your electricity and phone bill will make a big difference to your expenditure and therefore your bottom line. There are a glut of providers out there, desperate for more customers – so negotiate hard and remember that they need your business.

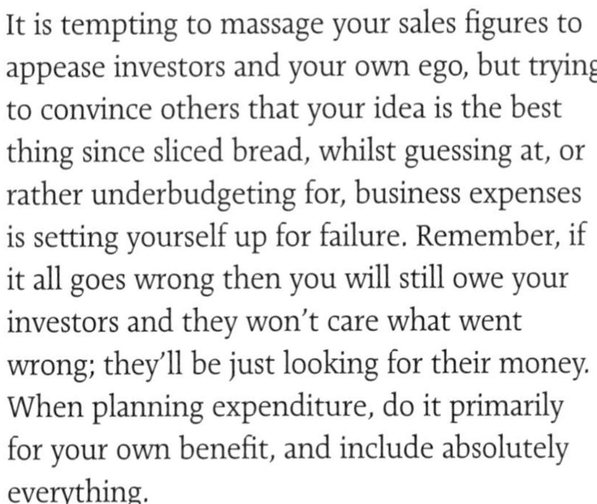

It is tempting to massage your sales figures to appease investors and your own ego, but trying to convince others that your idea is the best thing since sliced bread, whilst guessing at, or rather underbudgeting for, business expenses is setting yourself up for failure. Remember, if it all goes wrong then you will still owe your investors and they won't care what went wrong; they'll be just looking for their money. When planning expenditure, do it primarily for your own benefit, and include absolutely everything.

Your wage bill will always be your largest outgoing, closely followed by your stock – though if you are a service rather than a product provider, then you have slightly more room for manoeuvre. Although including these costs into your projections is absolutely key, ensure that you add on the other costs that every business faces – and find out exact figures, never rely on a rough guess. The surprise costs that start making a hole in your finances are all the ancillary costs. Look at how much electricity you will be using both when

you are working in the business premises and when the place is dormant. A massive cost for small businesses is paper and ink – whether it be copying, printing or scanning, it all adds up. Postage should be a major concern no matter what type of business you are planning to launch, and then the shock of running an internet connection, water, phones, rates and machinery all rear their ugly heads.

Even the big bills are not set in stone. Whatever salaries you are planning to pay, add on about 15% to cover the cost of employee NIC and PAYE in the UK, not to mention health, pensions, gym membership and travel loans, if these are perks you are considering for your staff. The more accurate you can be with the true expenditure your business will incur, the more accurate your projections will become. These bills are constant and spread evenly throughout the year. Even if the business you are starting is seasonal, you must still leave enough, and budget, to cover the monthly or quarterly barrage regardless of your own sales performance.

Try another idea...

Getting the numbers right, or at least on target, is difficult enough, but it is all wasted unless the results are presented in a sensible and effective manner. To learn more, check out IDEA 8, *Number crunching*.

Defining idea...

'Annual income twenty pounds, annual expenditure nineteen six, result happiness. Annual income twenty pounds, annual expenditure twenty pound nought and six, result misery.'

CHARLES DICKENS

How did it go?

Q Each of the providers is offering pretty much the same deal on the services we require. Considering that Company X is already supplying the premises, it makes sense to keep them on. Are we right to leave everything as it is?

A Maybe they are the best provider for your business and the last occupants did the hard work of shopping around. But remember, it is a competitive world and informed consumers holds the power in their hands. Explain to the current provider that you would dearly like to let them continue their service provision, but you really need to see how it is going to benefit you; you will be amazed at the special offers the sales rep suddenly remembers. Remember you are the customer and you are not going to be messed around.

Q We want to plan three years in advance but are finding it difficult to estimate expenditure that far ahead. Should we just guess at the numbers?

A Three years is not all that far away. Although your capital expenditure will not be as high, you will have to provide for any additional staff costs and an increase in liabilities such as power, phones, postage and advertising. Spend as much time working out your expenditure in year three as year one. Don't guess.

7

That's so 'des res'

***Location, location, location*, so the old maxim goes, and there is nothing more true about retail businesses – but location may not be as important if you are launching a non-retail business.**

You'll be spending an awful lot of time in your new premises. Forget the fancy blinds and funky lighting: what are the toilet and kitchen facilities like?

Retail businesses are completely dependent on you securing a good location and constant customer footfall. There is no room for manoeuvre and any compromise on the most suitable location will drastically affect your sales and ultimately the success of the business. Because rental prices for retail premises are tied into the footfall for an area, the temptation is to take the cheaper (and maybe larger) premises and hope that advertising, word of mouth and reputation brings the customers through your doors. This simply does not happen. You will be preaching to unhearing ears and spending a fortune in the process. If you want your business to be successful, give yourself a fighting chance.

Here's an idea for you...

Assuming that there are good communications in the vicinity, extend your search for suitable premises to a 40 km radius from your ideal location. The difference in the price, size and look of a place changes wildly with broader parameters. We all would prefer to work in nice, airy surroundings, even if it adds twenty minutes to our journey.

SIZE MATTERS

They say it doesn't, but it does. When considering how much space you need to rent or buy, you need to be looking at three scenarios: the space you require to set up and get the business off to a start; the space you will need if your growth is in line with your business plan; and the space you will need if things aren't quite as buoyant as you had hoped. Most rental agreements will be for far longer than you would wish. It is imperative that you are allowed to either break contract (probably with a financial penalty) or that you are allowed to sub-let. The worst situation is to be forced to stay in premises that are either too small or too big for your purposes, and then being forced to be paying for the upkeep of two premises.

Although every business is unique and will have space requirements particular to its particular needs, the trick is to allow for some growth but not to overstretch yourself. In the case of retail premises, ensuring that there is at least some space for stock outside the public area of the shop is imperative, especially to cope with seasonal needs. For industrial or commercial premises, look for premises that have at least one area of privacy that would be suitable for conducting meetings or private conversations – not the shop floor or someone's office.

PROJECTING AN IMAGE

If you're starting a business which doesn't involve customers coming to your premises very often, don't be tempted to buy or rent expensive pretty premises – it will be a complete waste of money. There really isn't anyone to impress and your money will go so much further if the location is a little less desirable or slightly off the beaten track. Obviously, if you're intending the public to enter the premises then the image of the building can be as important as the look you achieve inside, but don't get too carried away as an ostentatious premises can work against you, especially with investors looking to see how well you manage your (and potentially their) money.

Try another idea...

Once you have located and secured your premises, there will always be lots to do before you will ready to begin operations and show yourself off to the world. To learn more, check out IDEA 9, *Just needs a lick of paint.*

The rental price or sale price is only one of many charges associated with taking on premises for your business. As well as having to pay council tax, research how much you will be charged in management fees for the building or industrial estate, if you have to pay for rubbish to be collected, your responsibility for maintaining the property and if you are able to get the facilities you may require (such as broadband and security) to function. Insurance may be a huge cost if the premises have a history of break-ins and the businesses surrounding your premises can have an effect if there are concerns about safety.

Defining idea...

'The higher the buildings, the lower the morals.'

JOHN M. FORD, US author

How did it go?

Q We are launching a design company and location is important, but all we can find for the money are tiny properties that will make life very cramped. If we compromise, we might have more space but possibly no clients. Which property should we go for?

A *Location is important in industries such as design, but it is always better to have suitable premises in which you can work effectively over something that is far too small, terribly pretty, but absolutely impractical. Take the larger, less trendy premises and use the better facilities to create design masterpieces that will win you clients – not some pretty bricks near the docks.*

Q We plan on it taking about a month to find suitable premises and a month to get everything ready for launch. Is this realistic?

A *No! It can take many months to organise a lease on commercial premises and more to get them fit for your business needs. Give yourself as much time as possible and bank on about twelve weeks from first seeing a property to actually getting the keys. Fitting out can take even longer, especially for retail premises. Save time by researching and budgeting the fitting out process before you sign a lease. Look for bargains – good secondhand office furniture can save you a fortune.*

8

Number crunching

Many of us fear numbers, or see working with them as a terrible chore, but working accurately with spreadsheets will quickly show you, and others, if a business is viable.

These financial documents can be a prophetic vision of your financial future; when the hard graft is over each month, those figures you have entered under salary will be your reward.

When creating your financial spreadsheet, you really should be looking to prepare for every possible eventuality that you can foresee over the next three years. Even if your business is going to be in an office or a shop and you are looking to run a transactional website as a bit of a sideline, it could be that web sales will be your major route to market in eighteen months' time. Create a row for each and every route to market, even if you are projecting sales to be zero for the first year. Include everything like bank interest rates for loans and overdrafts, even if you are self-funding the business at launch – you may have a bank loan in the future and it is much easier to alter the rate of interest and enter an amount that you will be paying every month than it is to create a new spreadsheet.

Here's an idea for you...

Create a spreadsheet to present the following data as a graph:

- **Sales projections for the next twelve months**
- **Sales projections for the next three years**
- **Expenditure since launch**
- **Monthly bank balance for the next twelve months**

This should show you how easy it is to produce good visual data and make it clear where you should be in twelve months.

BREAK IT DOWN

As well as preparing for all foreseeable eventualities, it is good practice to be as specific as possible with your financial projections. If you are launching a hairdressing salon employing experienced stylists and apprentices, there will be different rates charged to the customers and differences in the cost of sales. Keeping your entire sales figures in one row makes it hard to analyse profits. It is better to create a row for each type of sale. Although the volume of sales through the stylists may be high value, your cost of sales (their salary or commission) is also going to be high. The apprentices will not charge as much for their work, but equally they will not be paid as highly, meaning more profit for the business – so it might prove better for your bottom line to employ one stylist and three apprentices than the other way around. The more information that you can present on your financial plans, the better you will be able to understand the full picture.

Defining idea...

'It is the responsibility of the sender to make sure the receiver understands the message.'

JOSEPH BATTEN, business guru

PRETTY PICTURES

Presenting the data can be done by simply printing off a copy of the spreadsheet – but very few people (apart from maybe an accountant) will be happy with this document.

Once the numbers are in, use the software to create more viewer-friendly versions and excerpts of the data. Graphs help readers 'picture' the business and understand the data far more easily than looking at an enormous spreadsheet. Although the viewer might need to refer back to the source document, your message can be displayed very quickly and accurately with a graph. Likewise, in your business plan you should summarise the data with simple one-line statements of fact or intent, e.g. 'with 47,000 investment we intend to create a business turning over 390,000 with a net profit of 61,000 within our first twelve months of operations.'

Try another idea...

To really get to grips with presenting financial data you must understand how to best manage business cash flow. To learn more, check out IDEA 32, *Peter paying Paul.*

When presenting data it is important to show when cash is actually going in and out of the business. If the rent bill is 12,000 per annum, display the outgoing funds, broken up into payments, as they will occur, not forgetting to account for deposits and legal fees. Managing cash flow will be the key to making your business a success. Find out what terms your suppliers offer, and *always* try to negotiate more favourable terms. Suppliers are often wary of new businesses – and rightly so, as so many go out of business leaving big debts unpaid. No matter how good your negotiation skills, some suppliers will demand a year of good relations before allowing more generous terms, or for the value of orders to exceed a certain level. The long-term goal is for your business to be selling products or services to your customers, and receiving the cash, before having to pay your suppliers.

Defining idea...

'It is a very sad thing that nowadays there is so little useless information.'

OSCAR WILDE

How did it go?

Q Our sales will be from client contracts for architectural designs; the values will fluctuate wildly depending on the size of the job. These figures don't make particularly pleasing graphs, so what should I do?

A *There is a lot that you can do to graphs to improve their appearance and shape. What this exercise is trying to show, no matter what business you are starting, is that your sales need to be higher than your expenditure, even if the revenue you receive varies wildly from month to month. But if, on paper, you do not expect the business to earn more money than it spends, you have a serious problem that no graph will be able to fix.*

Q Our projections show we fall short in year one, break even in year two and make a profit in year three. Will this hinder our plans for a loan?

A *This pattern is very common and no lender will be surprised to see a shortfall in year one. If the business is sustainable and profitability is possible in year three, you shouldn't have too much trouble in obtaining a loan, although you will probably have to provide security. Good businesses can run out of cash before they reach profitability, while bad businesses can pretend that profitability is always around the corner while continuing to spend money as if it is going out of fashion. The task for lenders and investors is to assess whether your projections are realistic.*

SAFETY
FIRST

9

Just needs a lick of paint

Image is everything, so the media would have us believe. There are very few shops and offices still operating that do not subscribe, in one way or another, to good presentation.

Err on the side of caution when choosing how you present yourself – chrome and birch will always win over MDF and a few random screws you found in the shed.

It is becoming increasingly important that the business is defined and your mission explained through the decoration, fixtures and fittings you choose for your business, both to motivate your staff and to give consumers confidence.

Gone are the days when staff would not complain about working in below-standard conditions, with poor lighting and without clean air. Health and safety regulations make it law that you must provide a certain level of comfort for employees and customers. Consumers are used to choice and high street chains have discouraged consumer loyalty – we shop with our feet, and if the environment is not to our

Here's an idea for you...

Compare prices between catalogues that are designed for a corporate consumer and those for domestic customers. It is likely that you can get the same or better products far cheaper as a domestic customer.

taste we will go elsewhere. Therefore, to become a serious player, you must subscribe to the image quest. The good news is that it need not cost the earth to give the impression of trendy, high-tech appeal. Many new businesses (mine included) are enjoying the prices of one particular Swedish furniture company and fitting their offices and shops out to a high specification at an affordable cost.

Getting your presentation right doesn't stop with furniture and fittings. The items that should be shown off are not your maple-finish desks or shiny clothes rails, it should be the stock itself. Clever window displays, sensible piles or shelves full of product can inspire sales as much as a good salesperson. In a retail outlet or online store you want the product to do the talking and the funky furniture to complement it, not steal the show. This is true of office environments also. Clients are meeting with you to see what your business can do for them. If they leave the meeting more impressed with your choice of corporate foliage and Italian coffee-maker than your ability to close the deal, it is all in vain.

There is still a lot of scope for being original. There is a homogenisation of both shops and offices which can be a bit bleak. Sometimes, breaking a little bit away from the norm is a good thing. Choose a theme and stick to it. As long as the overall effect is generally pleasing, it will speak volumes about the people running the business itself.

Defining idea...

'Nothing succeeds like the appearance of success.'
CHRISTOPHER LASCH, social critic

There is a lot to be said for getting stuck in yourself, when starting a business, especially on simple jobs. When launching a business, how far you can make your money go is absolutely critical. It is very easy to find all the tradesmen you require when you need work doing to a commercial premises. Prices can be double or triple that of the same job in a domestic setting, simply because they are billing a business. If your friends and family were a little reluctant to help financially with investment, they may be far more willing to pick up a paintbrush and help you get your premises ready for operation. If you have already hired, get all the staff involved to help you get the business off the ground – letting people feel empowered and involved will help morale and encourage responsibility.

Try another idea...

Once you have settled on the final look and feel of your premises, there is still a lot to be done in best presenting yourself and your business. To find out more, check out IDEA 11, *Looking like a tart.*

It may be something that you have or have not considered, but corporate work wear is a very successful way of helping encourage your brand and presenting your offering on a wider scale. Whether it is on full uniforms or just a polo-neck T-shirt, the name of your company will travel quicker, very cheaply. Although your staff are not likely to wear their company clothing over the weekend, they still have to travel to work and back, in public, wearing your logo.

Defining idea...

'The world is governed more by appearances than realities, so that it is fully as necessary to seem to know something as to know it.'
DANIEL WEBSTER, 19th century US politician

How did it go?

Q Flat-pack furniture is a lot cheaper, but isn't it likely to collapse under the wear and tear of an office or retail environment?

A *As with everything, if you pay peanuts you get monkeys. Remember, the overall quality of catalogue furniture and fittings has improved incredibly over the last decade. I am not suggesting buying the cheapest product on offer, but look to the higher-priced items, which will still be at least 25% cheaper than a commercial supplier. For items like flooring, you might still be safer buying industrial products because of the expected wear and tear, but a desk is just a desk.*

Q There is a local company that offers furniture leasing. Is this a good idea?

A *Not for a long-term project. You will be paying way over what the products are actually worth and you will be limited in choice as to what it is you can lease from them.*

Q I know that office suppliers charge over the odds, but isn't it a false economy to spend days, even weeks, running around looking for bargains?

A *It depends how much you plan to spend. If your budget is more than a week's wages, it is probably worth making the effort to save money.*

10

System addict

All businesses need to use machinery to save on time and expense. With the right systems in place, a single worker can do the job of many.

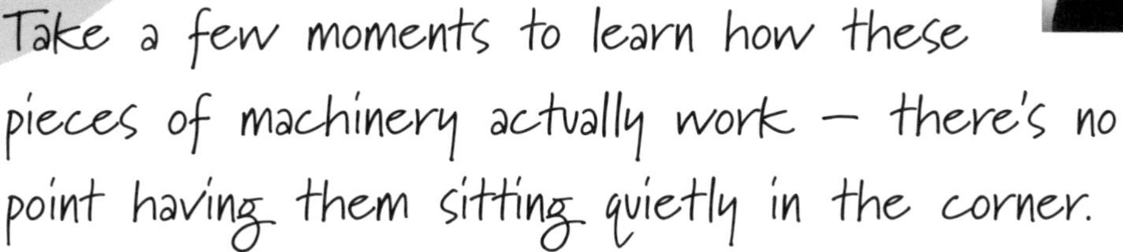

In this technical age it is highly unlikely that any business can survive without at least one PC. Personal computers empower you to put on any number of hats – from accountant to designer, from strategic planner to salesperson. With the right tools, you can do it all. Although there are other areas in which you can scrimp and save, the more that you can invest in technology, the larger your return. This is not to say you shouldn't still shop around for the best prices. Always try to buy the best specification machines. The growth of technology means that machines do get superseded quite quickly, and therefore, the higher up the bar you are at entry level, the longer it will be before everything needs to be replaced.

Here's an idea for you...

Create a document for yourself and future staff outlining the company procedure on backing up files. If your current PCs only contain a floppy drive and a CD burner, purchase an external storage unit for quick backups.

No matter what your thoughts are on the rise and influence of the internet, it is here to stay. It is very important that you and your staff are trained to use it well. As soon as you have premises, look into the broadband services for that area. Look at the higher end of what's on offer, for the cheapest price – especially deals that do not charge an installation fee or for the modem. Buy your domain name and set up a website (a holding page) to make your virtual presence known. It is essential to have at least one company email address – don't be tempted with a free web-based account (such as businessname@hotmail.com) because this will give the wrong impression of your business.

You also need more traditional forms of communication such as a phone system, fax machine and the all-important answer phone. Prices for these items are particularly low for reasonably high-spec systems. Although the internet should really have killed the fax, some of your suppliers or customers may still need you to be able to receive/send faxes. Don't disappoint or, worse, lose a sale, just for the price of a restaurant meal.

THE VIRTUAL FILING CABINET

What happened to all the information that used to take up filing cabinets in every room? Mostly it is now sitting on the hard drives of a few PCs – terribly neat, pleasing to the eye and all that extra space means a bigger office for you. But this is where the danger lies. When buying your business machines, the storage facilities you provide for your business are as important as the speed of the processor and the size of the hard drive. A huge hard drive is pointless if the machine is damaged or stolen – all of your records could be lost, with no way of ever recovering them.

Try another idea...

The business machines you buy in are pretty useless unless you complement them with the right software for your needs. To learn more, check out IDEA 44, *The soft machine.*

There are many storage solutions. The minimum you should have is a Zip drive that will allow you to store anywhere between 100 and 750 Mb on one single disk – for most computer users this is the entire contents of your C:\ drive and therefore every file, folder, email, image ever created or used on the system. The Zip disks can be backed up every day and stored securely off site.

GETTING PROTECTION

Be sure to investigate internet firewalls. Basic packages can be downloaded for free from the internet and even some operating systems such as Windows XP come with a firewall installed. Some network security should be created to stop employees (wilfully or by accident) downloading malicious files or viewing some content on the Web. Finally, protect your business by including a disclaimer on your outgoing emails stating that the views contained are those of the individual and, if the mail is received in error, it should be deleted.

Defining idea...

'Imagine if every Thursday your shoes exploded if you tied them the usual way. This happens to us all the time with computers, and nobody thinks of complaining.'

JEF RASKIN, creator of the Macintosh computer

How did it go?

Q Our business creates so few documents and they are so small that a few floppy disks can handle the entire process. We can save ourselves the expense of other storage solutions, can't we?

A *As soon as you become reliant on multiple floppy disks to store your information, you run a higher risk of data corruption, overwriting the wrong disk and, of course, losing a disk. An external Zip drive will cost about £70 ($120), which is hardly expensive for the peace of mind the facility gives you. A Zip disk is not only useful for backing up data – it can be used for saving large files, such as images, and sending them to clients or suppliers rather than clogging up their email for a day. It's also much quicker to put a file onto a Zip disk than burning it onto a CD-ROM.*

Q One of the directors thinks we should just back up to the server. Is this sensible? Couldn't something go wrong?

A *It is very sensible, and you will have the ability to back-up large amounts of information. Remember, though, that it is essential to ensure that the server is stored in a well-protected room, preferably off-site. It might be a good idea to make other forms of back up as well.*

Q What's a jump drive?

A *A flash stick, or jump drive, is a tiny storage device that plugs into your USB port. Currently they store between 128 Mb and 1 Gb, so a single stick can probably store all your text-based data. Try them – they're cheap!*

11

Looking like a tart

How you talk about the business, show figures and conduct yourself will all affect how your business is perceived by others.

From the moment that you start pitching the idea to friends and relations you should be looking to be able to capture the spirit of the business in just a sentence or two.

From now on you will be selling the idea of the business to others – be they investors, potential staff members or customers. You will find yourself repeating phrases that quickly become like politicians' sound bites. This is all healthy and normal and how most of us begin to learn the art of presenting. You are constantly being monitored and scored by the people around you on how well you present your business, even if at this stage it is just an idea.

The most important document that you will have to complete to get your business off the ground is a business plan and the associated financial data. Take sufficient time to complete these documents properly and put a lot of thought into how the

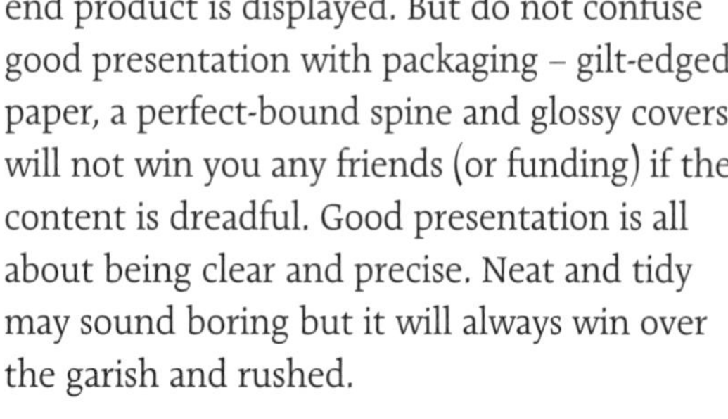

end product is displayed. But do not confuse good presentation with packaging – gilt-edged paper, a perfect-bound spine and glossy covers will not win you any friends (or funding) if the content is dreadful. Good presentation is all about being clear and precise. Neat and tidy may sound boring but it will always win over the garish and rushed.

By now you should have decided upon a name for the business and even a corporate logo. As soon as the logo or brand has been created, it is time to put it to work. Creating brand awareness is reliant upon people seeing references to you and your company repetitively – obviously a multi-million pound TV advertising campaign can create a brand very quickly, but most of us do not have that amount of money. Create corporate literature that is heavily branded with your logo. Create business cards for the staff who will be

Here's an idea for you...

Create an information pack suitable for potential investors, partners, suppliers and customers. The pack will be similar to an executive summary – showing what the business is setting out to achieve, the personalities behind it, pictures of the premises/product and some information about your target market. These packs allow you to leave a lasting impression with key contacts. The more succinct the information, the more effective it will be.

meeting clients and suppliers. Compliments slips are a way of presenting yourself well every time you send a package or free sample, and lastly, any official business correspondence should always be on headed paper. There is a time and a place for everything, and while very heavy and expensive paper does look and feel wonderful, it should really only be wheeled out for the special occasions.

There is always a line to be drawn between showmanship and frugality – customers and investors alike will be put off you and your business if it looks like everything is over-priced to keep you in the lifestyle to which you have become accustomed. Fancy cars, an over-jazzy office and an apparent easy-come attitude to spending money can give the impression of being wasteful rather than successful.

Try another idea...

Once you have created the printed material that is going to help you achieve your business objectives, you need to ensure that you and your staff are promoting the business in the right manner. To learn more, check IDEA 13, *What you think all the guns is for?*

Defining idea...

'What the public wants is the image of passion, not passion itself.'
ROLAND BARTHES

How did it go?

Q Over the past few weeks we have written the first draft of our business plan, but are not really sure what information to include in our information pack. Any ideas?

A *You are really looking to make a good first impression through clever marketing, not by producing a mini business plan. If you break the pack into five pages, page one would be an introduction to the business (name and logo) and relevant contact details (physical address, phone number/s and website address). Page two should include some statements regarding the products and/or services you will supply. Page three could include information about the business owners and directors/staff, including what makes you qualified to run this business. Page four could show your target market and why your business will appeal to them and page five could explain how you intend to reach them, by outlining your marketing plans.*

Q The marketing director would like to include a gift of some description. Is this wise or a bit tacky?

A *It can work, but it depends on the type of gift. As you want to get your brand recognised, it can be a good move to have some items such as pens or notepads with your brand showing through – think of practical products that people actually want to use on a daily basis. Leave a lasting impression. Avoid cheap calendars!*

12

Look at me!

You are one of many thousand new businesses launching this year; how do you ensure that you are heard above all the noise without spending a lot of money?

PR for your business should begin as soon as the business plan is finalised. There are many opportunities to start creating a buzz.

Even if there are still a few months to go before you have access to your premises or before you have finished fund-raising, you can still start promoting yourself. Start early by advertising for staff early. Often local papers can be persuaded to add some editorial to a job advert if you commit to them for all your recruitment advertising (this doesn't stop you using recruitment agencies). Try to get features written about you in the papers by showing how you are looking to recruit local talent and how this business is going to help the *local* economy grow.

Once the job vacancies are filled you have the opportunity to ask for a follow-up feature showcasing who has been employed. Any article written about your business should give you the chance to be able to show your logo and contact details.

Once the name of the business has been agreed, create the domain names that you require and start registering for free with the major search engines. The registration process can take six to eight weeks to come into effect. Internet job sites are a great

Here's an idea for you...

Any press releases you create should be tailored to the big nationals and sent to the relevant editor. You should also create a press release written for the trade press. By letting competing outlets and the industry suppliers know that you have arrived, you will make a strong first impression.

way to advertise any employment opportunities to a massive audience – ordinarily payment from you is only due if you accept the candidate.

Most cities and many towns have websites run or sponsored by the local council which include a business directory. It is well worth registering your business as it is yet another way that the public can find you on the net.

SAY CHEESE

Whether you like it or not, it is very much in your interests to be photographed – and this is true of all staff. By being photographed, you are much more likely to get the story or feature in the local papers because it gives the writer more angles to use in the story. With so many individuals and businesses fighting for PR, journalists are reluctant to plug a new business, no matter how cool or trendy it might be. By offering photographs and information about personalities, you can have a feature that is more of a 'lifestyle' story, but still answers the business' need to be noticed.

AND THE WINNER IS...

The public, it seems, never tires from entering competitions. The prizes on offer vary from the ridiculous to the impressive, but it seems not to deter them. With the aid of your local paper (or by paying for an insert), as you come closer to launching the business, offer some competition prizes by asking a simple question based on general knowledge or by providing the answer in 200 words of marketing blurb about the business. You are adding value to the paper and they will usually be quite warm to the idea, assuming that the value of the prizes is perceived to be quite high. Sometimes you might have to run the administrative side of the competition, but the knock-on effect is that you get a mailing list. Be sure to enter a note in the competition rules which states all entrants agree to be contacted in the future by you.

The moment that you have access to the business premises, be sure to erect some corporate signs. For a retail outlet this can cause a stir long before you have begun shop fitting and acquiring stock, and for commercial premises it announces your imminent arrival to surrounding businesses.

Try another idea...

Sometimes PR is not enough to get your message across. Advertising can be an expensive route to take, but can also reap rewards. To learn more, check out IDEA 36, *Buy it!*

Defining idea...

'Accustomed to the veneer of noise, to the shibboleths of promotion, public relations, and market research, society is suspicious of those who value silence.'

JOHN LAHR, theatre critic

How did it go?

Q Our business is a consultancy that will help other businesses get out of financial problems and run more efficiently. There isn't really a trade publication for us, so what can we do?

A Look at other organisations that may have members or clients that might need your services, such as the Institute of Directors. Be creative about possible publicity outlets. Getting PR for your business means letting as many people know about your business as you can – wherever they are – be they potential investors, suppliers or clients.

How did it go?

Q Can you issue too many press releases?

A *Not really. The worst that can happen is that only a few press releases are actually used and put into print and the others ignored. For the price of a stamp keep sending the news out.*

Q But people tell me that the big papers throw most press releases into the bin. What's the point in sending them something?

A *It helps to have an angle. Try to write a press release that gives some information or story that would be of interest to the specific paper you are sending it to. And try to send it to the right person – telephone first and try to find out what they are looking for. Supply good quality photographs, too.*

Q We don't seem to get anywhere with anyone except the local papers. What are we doing wrong?

A *Local papers are the easiest targets – they don't have much news! With other publications, you need to put in more thought. Try hiring a PR consultant who has a track record of getting good free publicity.*

13

What you think all the guns is for?

To make your business a success you must present yourself as the best person for the job in everything that you do.

Your confidence will rub off on those who read what you write and listen to what you say. Success comes from thinking successfully.

Having attitude does not only mean threatening behaviour, talking loudly about 9mm's, driving erratically and wearing far too much gold – that's just being silly. In business, attitude is all about having bags of confidence, not bling.

The image that all business owners must portray is confidence through their understanding of the business inside out. Customers, suppliers and investors will be far more likely to part with their money and products if they feel that they are giving them to a safe pair of hands. As an owner of the business, it is your absolute responsibility to be aware of what it is your business is trying to achieve, how you will achieve it and your own ability to manage the process. It is imperative that you

Here's an idea for you...

Rather than sending client- and media-facing staff on a professional course, prepare a five-minute speech for them yourself, and practise it first on friends and family. Find out if there are any seminars or conferences nearby that are looking for speakers – it could be good training for you.

Defining idea...

'He who establishes his argument by noise and command, shows that his reason is weak.'
MICHEL DE MONTAIGNE

quickly show understanding rather than arrogance and that you are not caught out by questions that you should know the answer to.

Tempers will be tested to their limit both during the preparation for the business and once it is launched. After all, you and your staff's livelihood is dependent on your business being successful; you should not be surprised if frustration shows at times. How you deal with surprises, crises and setbacks often determines your worth as someone suitable to launch a business, much more than how you react to success. It is important to curb your anger whenever possible and show to others that you are the right person to make it all happen. There is nothing worse than people having rows in public – and remember, your businesses premises are a public place.

When you are running your own business, certainly for the first few years of operation, you eat and sleep the business. There is no down time and the business will always be at the forefront of your mind. To make it harder, you will be expected to be on call by suppliers, customers and staff almost 24 hours a day, every day. Most people who start a new business find that they work far longer hours than they ever did when they were employees. Watch your diet and your health – you may need to take extra vitamins.

Try another idea...

For more on successful presentation and getting your message across, check out IDEA 22, *Presenting your future.*

Learn to accept that this is going to be the norm and to truly make the business a success you must be in a position to field calls or emails at unsociable hours – you will be pushed and pulled from all directions, but if it works and the business begins to grow in momentum and size, you will soon be able to delegate these tasks to specific members of staff and reclaim a little piece of your life.

Defining idea...

'It pays to be obvious, especially if you have a reputation for subtlety.'
ISAAC ASIMOV

Try to be cheerful all the time – and mean it! Make people feel happy to be around you, whoever they are. Make sure that you, and everyone else in the business, is sensitive to the needs of people who come into your premises, whoever they are. Don't let them stand around waiting while you fiddle with the photocopier, or worse, chat about the party last weekend. Be prompt, attentive and on the ball.

How did it go?

Q Even speaking in front of family and friends is a little nerve-racking when I am talking about the business. I can't possibly perform in front of investors or suppliers. Shouldn't I look after the planning and let others do the talking?

A *The ability to speak in public does not come to everyone naturally. You can either choose to remove yourself from proceedings completely and pass the responsibility on to another member of staff or business owner, or you can start to work on it. Suppliers and investors will be very keen to speak with you, especially when you are setting up the business. Choose locations such as your office or another familiar environment to make the meeting a little less nerve-racking. As with anything, practice makes perfect. The ability to communicate ideas is all very much part of assuming the right attitude to make your business succeed.*

Q I'm not nervous about speaking but I know that my delivery is poor. I have a strong regional accent and have to repeat myself a lot to be understood. Don't you think it would be better to hand the responsibility over to someone else?

A *Again, the more people who get to see and hear you talk about your business the better it will be for your future success. If you are going to let others talk, do turn up to the meeting for moral support and so that your clients, suppliers and investors can put a face to the name.*

14

Bank on it

Banks, we sometimes forget, are businesses looking to increase customers and profits – the same ideals as you've probably stated in your business plan.

Personal banking and business banking are two very different arenas, but there is a lot you can do to make sure that your business is enjoying a good service and a bit of personal attention.

Although a sawn-off shotgun will probably get you the cash you require, there is another way…Thankfully most banks do not try to tempt corporate customers with gimmicks and freebies, because they know it won't work. As a customer looking for a banking solution, *you* hold the power to take your banking wherever you please, based on hard facts: the charges. The charges that banks apply to business accounts vary from harsh to daylight robbery. Business banking is a cash cow. Don't be fooled by the glamorous welcome packs and glossy brochures; look at how much it costs to present a cheque, accept a credit card payment or transfer money by BACS or CHAPS. Banks can and do charge for merely opening an account or sending you a

Here's an idea for you...

Arrange an overdraft facility, even if you never intend to use it, rather than having to react to a cash-flow problem should it arise. Create a document that argues the case, explaining that it is better to prepare for all eventualities, and how the current arrangement is not related to the projected turnover of the business.

letter, and it's not cheap. In return, as a customer you are more likely to be able to arrange for a business loan or overdraft – but don't confuse this for benevolence; lending is also a way for banks to make lots of money, very fast, through the interest rate and terms they offer you.

On the bright side, banks provide a huge lifeline to businesses by offering a helping hand, especially in their formative years when it counts. Banks are very keen for your business to succeed because they will make money out of you for a very long time – in return for this expected 'loyalty', you are in a position to open an account on the understanding that you expect both a loan and an overdraft facility. Ordinarily you will be introduced to an account manager who will be assigned to your account. Charges for this service will vary, but it is very shrewd to befriend this person. Get them introduced to you and your business right from the start. Even if the business plan is at a draft stage, let them take a look and offer suggestions. The more exposure they have to your business and your thoughts, the more receptive they will be when it comes to giving you cash – be it loans, overdrafts or a reduction or waiving of fees. Your account manager will have you and many others on the books – ensure that you are their most exciting account.

BIDING YOUR TIME

A new business without any previous history is always at a disadvantage. No matter what figures are put on a spreadsheet, until you start trading and the bank is able to build a profile, lenders will be wary. However, no matter what opening loan or overdraft facility you are offered, within six months of trading a profile begins to form and you are able to look at your bank as a potential source of second-round funding. A bigger loan or overdraft facility is more likely to be granted once the business is set up and operating. Once the bank sees money coming in and out of the account, and you have shown your account manager the PR, advertising and CVs of key personnel you have attained since launch, all the odds begin to stack up in your favour. Show the bank that your business is really taking shape, along with detailed plans about how you intend to use the money, to the last pound, and justify why there is a sudden need for it now when there wasn't before. The bank will probably look for security on the loan. Make sure you are certain that the money will indeed lead to increased business – don't pump more good money after bad.

Try another idea...

Sometimes the amount you need to raise is too much for a bank to consider taking the investment risk. You might have to look towards business angels and venture capitalists for the money. To learn more, check out IDEA 15, *The Tet offensive.*

Defining idea...

'A banker is a fellow who lends you his umbrella when the sun is shining, but wants it back the minute it begins to rain.'

MARK TWAIN

How did it go?

Q The bank is reluctant to increase our overdraft until we have been trading for at least eighteen months. Is there any hope?

A *Banks may well ask for a history of account activity before agreeing to allow any more authorised borrowing, but often, if you are willing to drop the additional asking amount slightly, and mention that a rival bank seemed keen on agreeing to a similar figure, the argument is won. It's all about compromise and a little bit of nerve.*

Q We are worried that if we have a large overdraft facility, we will use it. Isn't the temptation to spend a little dangerous?

A *Not if your financial controls are in place and you stick to budget. Never look at the overdraft facility as spare money to dip into; it is there as a final option only, but it is better to have it arranged in advance. Remember, overdrafts are borrowed money, and quite expensive borrowed money at that. Use it to smooth cash-flow problems while you are waiting for debts to be paid – don't use it for investing in the business. In addition, an overdraft can be recalled unexpectedly, so make sure you pay it off regularly. Ideally you should not be overdrawn more than a few days each month.*

Q Should I remortgage my house or get a bank loan?

A *Mortgage loans are the cheapest money you will ever get – but watch the charges and penalties for remortgaging. If the sum you are borrowing is more than, say, a year's wages, then it is usually better to take the mortgage route because it is cheaper.*

15

The Tet offensive

Sometimes banks are unwilling to lend large sums of money, especially if the money is unsecured. This is when you need to call in the big guns.

To say dealing with venture capitalists or business angels is like selling your soul to the devil might sound a bit strong – but it's not far off...

If you require larger amounts to realise your business objectives, then a route to raising the capital could be through either business angels or venture capitalists. Business angels tend to be individuals looking to invest their money in new businesses, or businesses seeking a second round of investment to help growth. It all sounds incredibly benevolent, but angels want a better return than they would receive through a bank (currently approximately 5% p.a) or through investing in stock (currently 10–14% p.a.) and therefore will be *encouraging* you to make as much money as quickly as possible. Angels are usually found through business networks or online and often tend to invest only in businesses operating within a sphere of their expertise.

Here's an idea for you...

Wasting valuable time pitching to the wrong angel or VC is not going to help, as responses can take weeks if not months. Target those with a track record of investing in your industry. Once you have identified a short-list of potential investors, tailor your business plan accordingly – when and how much profits you are going to make. VC firms don't want the marketing fluff, they want the cold, hard figures along with an explanation about how you will make it happen.

Venture capitalists (VCs) tend to be corporate organisations that invest heavily in new businesses and like angels will be looking for a high return on their investment – quickly. Both angels and VCs will most probably want a share of the company in return for cash or a share of profits and will often insist on placing a few of their own people on the board. Accepting this level of funding does come with a price – the loss of some control – but by accepting their money you can often tap into their wealth of experience about all sorts of issues. After all, both types of investors will want to make sure your business succeeds.

Business angels can be just that: heavenly angels providing the capital to make an idea work and kick-start a business into an innovative, exciting and profitable enterprise. But this level of financial assistance does not come easily or cheaply. A business angel, or group of angels, is looking for a healthy *and safe* return on the investment that far outweighs the more obvious routes to letting money work for them – i.e. savings accounts and share dealing. To entice a business angel something must be so striking or unique about your offering that it really makes people sit up and take note. Opening a hairdressers is unlikely to attract this kind of investment, but an innovative software product or organisation that is trying to set new precedents with technology are very high up on the list.

Venture capitalists usually have significant amounts of other people's money to hand, over which they have free-reign (or certainly a lot of influence) to invest in businesses they feel are worth pursing. This is purely and systematically for financial gain. During the internet boom of the late 1990s, venture capitalists seemed more active than ever, with literally billions being pumped into internet-based businesses around the world. Some of these investments paid off tenfold, but a large majority failed to achieve any return whatsoever on the capital employed. The net effect was that venture capitalists pulled the plug on internet investments and started looking elsewhere.

Try another idea...

If you are looking for only a small amount of capital to finance your business, it is probably better to involve a bank. To learn more, check out IDEA 14, *Bank on it.*

Choosing the route of venture capitalist investment can be both good and bad for your business. In the short-term it can actually cost you money to look for investment because a lot of the charges, such as accountancy fees, legal fees and consultant rates, are borne by your business until the deal is done, in which case it is paid back. Therefore, this route of fund-raising is simply not viable for many businesses mainly because you need to have a large amount of disposable capital to spend in the first place.

Defining idea...

'Everybody likes a kidder, but nobody lends him money.'
ARTHUR MILLER

How did it go?

Q It looks as if it will take five years for our business to reach its potential and start pulling in serious amounts of profit. Will this deter a venture capital firm?

A *Every venture capital firm will have a different agenda, so there are no hard and fast rules. Although they are looking for a quick turnaround, in some industries five years is pretty quick. Don't let the timeline deter you. Prepare the data and the pitch to the best of your ability and look forward to a response. If you end up working with the VC firm closely, you will soon learn what sort of timeline suits them.*

Q The venture capitalist we approached is keen but insists we call him 'Lord Vader'. Is this allowed?

A *Call him Veronica if that's what floats his boat – just think of the cash!*

Q I thought that the best VCs are in America – shouldn't I try over there?

A *If your business is innovative and has the potential to be run in other countries, including the USA, it is not crazy to approach American VCs first. They have more access to capital and greater expertise than most VCs elsewhere. Some VCs have a reputation for demanding impossible deals that ensure that the owner loses their business if they are successful. Do your homework, and try to talk to people in the business; don't go automatically for the first deal that offers you some money.*

16

Status anxiety

Deciding upon the legal identity and status of your business can be tough, but remember, the status of a business can bring 'high status'.

Becoming CEO of a PLC does sound great, but floating a company is not always best for your business. Choose wisely and ensure that you remain in control.

LIMITED COMPANIES

The limited company is regarded as the best thing that the Victorians ever did for us, although I would argue that the flushing toilet was equally important. A limited company is a completely separate legal entity from those who run or work for the company (thus the directors have limited liability). With that definition come a number of benefits and disadvantages.

By creating a limited company you can give the impression of size and experience very easily, even if the business is completely new. Customers will be happier writing cheques to XYZ Ltd. than to John Smith. However, some suppliers are less keen for small companies to be limited because it can give the impression that you

Here's an idea for you...

Take the time to speak with an accountant to help you decide which status best suits your own business. Your accountant will be able to advise on which status will help you achieve your long-term goals as well as recommending which is best at this stage to help minimise your tax and VAT liability. These are huge decisions and not to be made on the spur of the moment.

are protecting yourself from risk, which ironically makes you a risky bet. Banks tend to feel the same and in a bid to ensure that any money they lend to a business is in some way protected or secured, will ask the directors to sign a mandate ensuring that if the business is unable to meet repayments, you as directors will. In the UK, filing accounts with Companies House is a legal requirement if you become a director of a limited company and there are knock-on costs if you require your accountant to prepare these documents for you.

PARTNERSHIP OR LIMITED LIABILITY PARTNERSHIP

A partnership works for a number of industries and types of businesses exceptionally well, and not so well for others. The classic examples of partnerships are law firms and accountancy firms. With a standard partnership the partners have unlimited liability and this means you would be liable for the business debts of your partners even if you were unaware of the debt. There are, however, tax advantages to forming a partnership. A recent invention is the limited liability partnership, which is almost a fusion of partnership and limited company in that the partners enjoy the protection of limited liability but remain partners rather than directors.

SOLE TRADER

A sole trader is on the bottom rung of the status ladder. With that come quite a few benefits and a few disadvantages, but most importantly it speaks volumes about the perceived 'size' of your business – which can work both for and against you. A sole trader has unlimited liability and so is responsible for all the debts of the business; however, more and more large firms are happy to deal with sole traders because they appreciate the risk that the individual is taking and feel they are more likely to get a good service and value for money.

Try another idea...

For more about dealing with accountants check out IDEA 18, *Enjoying the anal retentive.*

PLC

Going public is often seen as the king of the status pile – 'publicly owned' immediately conjures images of size and access to capital, even though the truth of the matter may be far different. PLCs work very well for creating a buzz and interest in your company, but with the extra cash raised from the flotation and shareholders come your commitment to being scrutinised and having to appease shareholder sentiment and the need for return. It is important to understand that the shareholders own a PLC, not the directors of the business. You could be voted off the board, but equally you could be managing director of a multi-million pound international conglomerate far quicker than through running a partnership or limited company.

Defining idea...

'A static hero is a public liability. Progress grows out of motion.'
RICHARD BYRD, explorer

How did it go?

Q We have decided to form a limited company in the UK. The accountant wants us to 'buy one off the peg'. Is this advisable?

A *Yes, this means that a company has been formed at Companies House and all you need do is pay the money (about £250) and change the name of the company to one of your own choosing. At a push, and for a fee of about £100 extra, this can all be done in the same day.*

Q If we form a PLC will our share price be quoted on the FTSE next to ICI and all the other big boys?

A *Probably not. Your nominated broker will decide when and where to float the company. If you are based in the UK then this will most likely be on the Alternative Investment Market. The AIM is a specific market for smaller, growing companies. Company flotation is extremely expensive, and all the middlemen (the brokers and investment bankers) want to ensure both that they make their fees and that the company lasts long enough for them to get rid of any shares they have underwritten and be free of criticism should the firm collapse later. That makes them very reluctant to get involved with any business that does not have a good track record and very professional management. In general, seeking to float a company is not something you should consider until you have been trading successfully for several years and can show that you have a huge growth potential.*

EMail
WWW
Stocks
CLR

17

Just give me my phone call

Going it alone is very risky when it comes to launching a new business. Bring a solicitor in on your project as soon as possible.

Solicitors charge for their services but they look out for you and your interests. Employing a solicitor to help you get started will be far cheaper than employing one should you get into legal difficulty later.

Before you buy or lease property for the business, be sure to request a land registry search through your solicitor. Although everything might look fantastic on the estate agent's information sheet, they are only acting on the word of the vendor, and not everything may be true. The search will reveal important information about access, by-laws, parking and if the property is sitting on any dodgy radioactive pockets of gas. Most importantly it will confirm that the person asking for the money is indeed entitled to sell or lease.

Here's an idea for you...

To fully appreciate the worth of employing a solicitor for the business, test their skills by requesting a standard staff contract particular to your industry. For a single fee you will now have a company contract, which can be simply altered for every employee you hire. As you will have to issue yourself a contract if you become a limited company, this is money well spent.

Solicitors have template contracts available at the touch of a button. Unless your company is employing permanent legal staff or happens to have a qualified lawyer on the board, this information and their knowledge of current law is absolutely vital to your business and continued good relations with your staff. Employing somebody to work for a business is more of a commitment than it has ever been. Staff obviously help bring the business to life and help you achieve your goals; they're also your most expensive drain on resources. In a small business this can cause all sorts of problems, not least of which is long-term illness. Protect yourself and your staff with a bona fide contract of employment.

If you plan to launch a website it is paramount that you have a legal statement on the site. The pages should cover your contractual agreement with users and their agreement when using your site. Is it clear who owns the copyright on text, images and other content found on your site? It is well worth the cost of having a legal expert read over your statement. Pinching another website's statement and altering it to suit you own needs is not good enough – you will be caught out either by the originator or by a user finding loopholes.

'Put more trust in nobility of character than in an oath.'
SOLON, ancient Greek lawmaker

It will quickly become apparent during the creation of a business plan that you are likely to need the services of a law firm. Depending on the need and the cost, it might be wise to set up a fixed monthly or quarterly payment that is offset against their invoices. The monthly charge will be easier to manage and much better for cash flow than reacting to varying sized bills as and when they are presented. The firm itself will be able to suggest a suitable amount – if it is incorrect you will both soon realise and the situation is easy to resolve.

Try another idea...

As well as the services of a solicitor, you are going to need to deal with an accountant to get your business up and running. To learn more, check out IDEA 18, *Enjoying the anal retentive.*

To build up a good working relationship fast, it is well worth putting any private work you might have through the firm of solicitors you plan to use for the business. Something simple, like a will, will cost you very little, and is something that you should have organised anyway. Because you have a number of reasons to call, your name will soon register with the solicitor and, sometimes more importantly, her secretary; if you do need to talk urgently you are far more likely to be top of the list of messages, not bottom.

Defining idea...

'Lawyers, I suppose, were children once.'
CHARLES LAMB

How did it go?

Q My solicitor is based miles away from where we are setting up the business. Is this going to be a problem?

A *Probably not, in that most of the documents your solicitor will be working on will not require your presence. Do allow sufficient time for post to go both ways if you are dealing with a solicitor based in another town or city, though.*

Q Both our solicitor and our accountant have offered to set up the limited company for us. Is one better than the other for this purpose?

A No, they will both be completing the same forms on your behalf. Go with the cheapest – which may well be the accountant.

Q My solicitor always seems to create more problems, and refuses to tell me how much a job is going to cost. Should I find another solicitor?

A This is a common problem. To be fair to the legal profession, it is difficult for them to know how much work will be needed on a given task, and part of their job is to think of potential problems that you haven't considered. Clients always want firm answers, but often fail to understand the issues involved. A solicitor cannot answer questions like, 'Will I win this case?' with a definite 'yes' or 'no' – it all depends...

Q My partner says it is always better to avoid a lawsuit. Is this true?

A Lawsuits cost a great deal of money, so unless your pockets are very deep this is probably a good principle. Certainly, in many cases it is far better to settle out of court or to write off a loss than to embark on an expensive court case that takes years.

18

Enjoying the anal retentive

Accountants are highly skilled individuals. Getting the right one will save you and your business hundreds or thousands a year. Get the wrong one and you will be paying through the nose for bad, even dangerous, advice.

If you don't get a buzz out of crunching numbers, don't worry, these people do. They might not be much fun at the Christmas party but they will make sure you can afford to have one.

Many businesspeople regard accountants as though they are the enemy. This is not the case if you have a good working relationship with an accountancy firm. Very few of us like working with numbers (those who do are accountants!) but it is an intrinsic part of running and operating any business. A good accountant is on your side to ensure that the business is able to make, and more significantly keep, as much profit as possible – and this is not a bad thing. A good accountant needs to be brought in right from the start, to get to know you and the proposed business right from its infancy. You will not be scored badly for offering an incomplete plan, just

Here's an idea for you...

Make a shortlist of three firms who you would consider employing as your accountants. Prepare your questions and meet with each. The firm that is most keen for your business should be your first choice. Over the coming years they will be charging you for their services, so make them earn their money right from the first meeting.

helped in the right direction to make it right. By allowing accountants to give you feedback on early drafts of the business plan, they quickly learn about what it is you are trying to achieve and can tailor their service to suit you and the company – saving you needless meetings and expenditure.

Accountants come in all shapes and sizes. Choosing an accountant is a major decision, so you should never just reach for the telephone directory and pick a name that sounds quite good. As a rule of thumb, don't contact firms that advertise in the local papers, or who drop flyers through your door, or worse, who cold call you – although they have every right to advertise, it does beg the question 'why do you not have enough clients?' The best way to choose a firm of accountants is through personal recommendation. If someone you know runs a business and they've been happy with their accountant for a few years, it's a safe bet that they will work well for you too. Unlike solicitors, it also pays to use a local firm. Not only will you get a more personal service, it will be much better when it comes to preparing the company accounts if you are able to transport files and documents by hand or car than trusting them to the mail.

Defining idea...

'It is better to know some of the questions than all of the answers.'
JAMES THURBER

A good habit to get into from the moment you start planning your new business is to keep records of absolutely everything. An organised office is immediately obvious from the number of box files taking up every available shelf. Leave nothing to chance. You can always destroy it in a year's time if it really is useless. As a bare minimum, every business should have a box file for:

- Bank statements
- Credit card statements
- Invoices received
- Invoices issued
- Staff (contracts and income tax information)

Try another idea...

Along with the services of an accountant, you are also going to require a solicitor to assist you in creating and maintaining your business. To learn more about the role of solicitors, check out IDEA 17, *Just give me my phone call.*

There really is no upper limit on the number of box files you use over the coming years, but happy indeed is the accountant who can ask for a document and the client knows exactly where to look!

Accountants vary enormously in the methods they use to produce your accounts. Remember, there is no single correct answer in accounting issues. In general, they prefer to understate profits rather than overstate them because optimistic accounts tend to lead to more problems later. You can picture the scenario: gung-ho businessman puffs his accounts, borrows money and attracts investors, and finally, a few years later, goes broke. Who does everyone blame? The accountant, of course! Every time there is a big business scandal, from Robert Maxwell to Enron and Worldcom, the accountants are brought shuffling out to explain how they allowed the managers to bamboozle them. From an accountant's point of view, a 'conservative' attitude towards profits is highly desirable – and it means you pay less tax, too.

How did it go?

Q We met with a number of accountancy firms and we got on least well with the firm that seem the most qualified to assist with our business. Should we choose personality over experience?

A *No. You won't have to talk to your accountant every day, or every week for that matter. If an accountant has worked with businesses similar to yours in the past, then they will hit the ground running. The fact that you find the person a little abrasive or unpleasant won't stop them doing the job well.*

Q A friend of mine is training to become an accountant. He has offered us a great deal if we use him. Is this wise?

A *If he or she has not yet qualified yet, you will be risking your business and possibly your livelihood. Pay the premium and employ someone who is already qualified – you can always change accountants at a later date.*

Q My chartered accountant comes to my office and finishes everything in two sessions. My friend has a similar small business and he says he has to take a week off each year to prepare the books in the way the accountant wants them. What is going on?

A *Perhaps you just naturally keep better records than your friend! Accountants do vary a lot in their style. If your friend is being forced to prepare figures in a way that seems unreasonable, perhaps he could ask a different accountant how they would expect the information to be presented.*

19

Friend and enemy

It might be your leadership and direction that drives the business initially, but it will be your staff members who are responsible for realising the dream.

Staffing your business with all of your mates from the pub will make you very popular, but unless you are planning to run a pub, it really is a bad move.

Hire the right person for the job and it can only mean success; get it wrong and it could collapse the business. Naturally, the first people you will turn to in your hour of need are your friends and family. You will no doubt be aware of their present circumstances, salary and job satisfaction – which is an awful lot of information and allows you to offer an alternative package and working conditions to win them over.

Employing friends and family can be the best move you and your business can make. You already know about their reliability, timekeeping and sickness record and there is a good chance that you will get more for your money in terms of number of hours worked and quality of work. On the flip side, there is also a very good chance that it can all backfire spectacularly, and then you are left with the worst of all decisions: how do you get rid of them?

Here's an idea for you...

Go through the interview process even if you are employing a relative or friend whom you have known for years. You will be able to explain the aims and objectives of the business and the ground rules regarding timekeeping, professional conduct and dress code in the manner in which you intend to run the business. Unless you actually tell someone what you expect of them, they will not deliver.

Make sure you are familiar with your rights and responsibilities as an employer before you hire anyone. In particular, write down clear, detailed job descriptions and give them to potential employees along with their contract of employment. The job description helps to focus everyone's attention on what is required, and can be very useful if there are subsequent disputes.

RECRUITMENT AGENCIES

Recruitment agencies perform a valuable service and expect to be paid accordingly. The charges vary wildly depending on your location, industry and the level at which the job is advertised. Using an agency often does result in your business being staffed by the right person, very quickly, but it comes at a cost. Don't feel any loyalty, advertise the role with as many agencies as possible, and take the position off their books if an agency continues to send unsuitable applicants.

WEBSITE

You really should have a website to both advertise and showcase your business. If there are services or products that can be sold via the internet, then you are probably doing this already. The moment that a vacancy for employment is on offer, it is always best to try and attract the right candidates yourself. Adding a jobs page to your site is incredibly cheap and can be highly effective.

ADVERTS

Placing adverts for positions vacant can be an expensive option, but if you are able to write and place well-written adverts in well-targeted locations, then the savings and quality of applicant can be very good indeed. The level of the position will quickly make it obvious where you really need to be advertising. Local papers do serve a function, but only really up to a certain level. The national newspapers are expensive but their penetration, assuming you research the paper's readership and themes, can prove to be one single payment resulting in a plethora of interest, all from good candidates.

Try another idea...

To convince your staff that your business idea is going to work should be as important as, if not more so, than convincing customers. To learn more, check out IDEA 22, *Presenting your future*.

PRETTY TO LOOK AT, NOT MUCH GOOD

Don't be tempted to hire someone for their pretty/handsome face if you think his or her skill set is lacking. Whilst for most of us it is nice to be surrounded by beautiful people, at the end of the day you are employing staff to work for your business, not give you an ego trip.

Defining idea...

'Furious activity is no substitute for understanding.'

H.H. WILLIAMS, lawyer and author

How did it go?

Q We are so busy getting everything prepared for the launch it seems a bit counter-productive to timetable an interview. Can't this wait until we get a quiet moment in a few weeks' time?

A *There are no quiet moments with new businesses and it really is unwise to hold an interview for the position weeks or months after someone has been working in the role. Just thirty minutes will do it and it's another tick on the list.*

Q My cousin is notoriously bad at getting out of bed in the mornings but I know that once he gets into work he'll make up the hours. I don't want to rock the boat at this early stage and I need all the help I can get. What should I do?

A *No other employer would tolerate late mornings; either he arrives on time for the working day (whatever those hours are) or he finds employment elsewhere. If you are lenient with one member of staff, it will strain relations with other members very quickly.*

Q I have one very talented potential employee who wants to work from home most of the time. She says she doesn't need to come in more than one morning a week. What should I do?

A *If you can agree on a way for measuring her output, why not let her organise things the ways she wants? As long as she does the work, does she really need to be in the office all the time?*

20

Whose baby is this?

Becoming a limited company or a PLC does mean giving up some of the overall control of the business, but it gives you more people who you can call on for advice.

Don't feel that you must have a long mahogany table and chairs with tall backs to run a company, but if you have them and there's a white Persian cat on your lap, people will listen...

The chairperson is there to chair official meetings and to be, on occasion, the mouthpiece of the business. More often than not one of the directors acts as chair for the purpose of the board meeting; in some, mainly larger, organizations, there is a permanent chair. The chairperson controls who speaks and for how long they speak in official meetings and, if there is a hung vote, he or she has a casting vote. Choose a chairperson who is looking after the interests of the business, not their own or their cronies' need for a power trip.

How the other directors perceive and receive the managing director of an organisation always makes for interesting board meetings. The managing director, ordinarily, is appointed to the board and employed by the company to manage the day-to-day operation of the business. Managing directors are usually brought in by

Here's an idea for you...

Choose a director from another sector. Don't think that a director necessarily needs to have experience of your particular industry. In fact, it is often both useful and refreshing to have a new 'outside' voice come into the equation to address a particular failing and offer a radical solution.

the board to serve that purpose, and are also removed by the board if the need arises. Sometimes the managing director is the founder of the company and brings in other directors to form the board. There is no right or wrong way to do this, but these two scenarios make for two very different businesses.

In the case of the employed managing director, it is the board's responsibility to measure the performance of the company and to use the board meeting as a way to offer advice and place pressure on the management if performance is less than satisfactory.

In the case of the self-appointed managing director, although the board has the same powers, because they were brought in to fulfil a role, there is usually lots of advice offered but seldom much criticism.

Whatever the scenario, the board of directors should have good experience of the products and services being sold and should offer their advice freely and candidly. Equally, any criticism should be heeded by the managing director and efforts made to rectify the problem. If the managing director is able to ignore advice and criticism and continue in the role, the board meetings do not serve a useful function.

Defining idea...

'The only thing worse than a man you can't control is a man you can.'
MARGO KAUFMAN, US author and columnist

THE BOARD'S ROLE

Every management team requires support, advice and backing from the board of directors – within most businesses this is forthcoming. Being an effective director of a company should not mean turning up to the quarterly meeting and grilling the managing director for the sake of it. It is much better if the directors play a more active role in the firm's operations throughout the year, offering words of wisdom and, if need be, criticism on a regular basis rather than saving it all up for a two-hour onslaught at an annual board meeting. Do explain to your board what it is you require from them, otherwise you might all be working in the dark.

Try another idea...

In certain cases it makes good business sense to work with another individual or organisation to help realise your ambitions. To learn more, check out IDEA 26, *Selling out before you have begun.*

An oft-overlooked process that should always be completed whether you are looking to form a board of directors or whether the board already exists is to perform a skills audit, to see clearly where the business strengths and weaknesses lie within the management team. It is inevitable that some weaknesses will become apparent, and this is perfectly normal. The correct response is to try and address the shortfall, usually by taking on an additional director or manager who brings those exact skills to the business.

Defining idea...

'Watch out for the fellow who talks about putting things in order! Putting things in order always means getting other people under your control.'
DENIS DIDEROT, philosopher

How did it go?

Q Not a single member of our management team has any financial experience – we are all salespeople. Will we have to pay our accountant to join our board?

A *Not necessarily. There are 'board banks' all over the UK that supply very able and experienced directors to small businesses. Your local Chamber of Commerce should be able to put you in touch with them. You can choose the director you want with the skills you need.*

Q Is it possible to not pay anything to the directors?

A *It is fine not to pay directors for their time or advice on business matters, but it is a courtesy to cover their expenses for board meetings – and a cup of tea and a biscuit wouldn't go amiss either.*

Q One of my partners wants to bring a retired employee from a multinational onto the board. He was in personnel, and I think the appointment would be inappropriate; he just talks and doesn't seem to have much business sense. What should I do?

A *'Personnel'? He must have retired a long time ago – they call it 'Human Resources' now. You may be right in thinking that he has little to offer a small business; large corporations operate in a completely different way, so you always need to make sure that people with a background in multinational companies really do bring useful skills to the table – finance, logistics and marketing, for instance.*

SEVEN KEYS TO SUCCESS
* key is knowledge

21

Magnum opus

Creating a business plan is like baring your soul to the world because what is contained within the text will expose your aims, goals, aspirations and level of motivation for all to see.

Write the document for you, not others, and use it as the blueprint to success. Remember you're not writing a novel – less of the flowery prose and idealistic diatribe and more on the facts and figures.

A great business plan is really simple. No matter how complex your business, the end product should give any reader, no matter what their background, a huge insight into the business, your market, your goals and how you intend to succeed. A business plan should not be an excuse to confuse and wow readers with excessive use of management talk, industry lingo and overwhelming statements – it should outline your intentions in plain language. In terms of length, the business plan need only be as long as it takes to explain the proposition. Don't set yourself a page count and work towards that – write the plan, and if anything try and edit it down to 75% of the original size. A very long document will not help in raising funds, or

Here's an idea for you...

Before embarking on your business plan, obtain as many actual business plans as possible. Although there are no hard and fast rules about layout and style, as you begin to compare you will begin to see patterns. Use existing plans as a template.

encourage staff, or prove to be particularly useful in the future. In fact you will just bore people and maybe convince them that you are hiding insecurities about the business behind reams of stats, figures and a few poems thrown in for light relief.

Business plans really do reveal all, namely your own company's strengths and weaknesses, and are highly confidential documents that are not for public consumption. Be very careful who gets to see it and understand fully why a certain person needs to see it. Be sure to number each version and destroy older versions so that confusion does not arise.

A business plan is not a marketing document only comprising of forward-looking statements that will be nigh on impossible to achieve. A business plan is a working document, one that a good business refers back to again and again. It should lead your business to success and be followed, not locked in a filing cabinet once the seed capital has been secured.

What readers are looking for in a business plan is to be taken on a journey, from start to finish, of how you are going to make this business work. It's all very well concentrating on how many units you plan to sell and at what price, but don't lose sight of the fact that whatever industry you are planning to work in will have established competition. Acknowledge the competition and show categorically that you have researched the market. List your competitors' strengths and weaknesses.

If you are able to obtain financial data (try the annual shareholder reports), quote this and show where your business fits into the market.

Try another idea...

All good business plans begin with an executive summary. To learn more check out IDEA 23, *The language of lords.*

When planning how you are going to tackle the marketing aspect of the business, don't just list what you intend to do, work out a timeline (for yourself more than for others) and give people a point of reference of when certain projects or campaigns will begin and how long they will last. Break down the costs for each individual campaign and explain the rationale behind the expenditure and timing.

When the plan is complete you will need to test it on someone you trust but who is not involved in the business or the same industry. Can it be read and understood by someone completely removed from the business? Whatever terminology or areas they find difficult to understand must be revised or explained – your plan must have universal appeal.

Once complete and fully edited it is time to make sure that the plan itself is well presented. Nobody is expecting gilt-edging, but having the document bound, or at least placed in a colour co-ordinated folder, will make you and your proposal all the more attractive – and the reader is also less likely to lose random pages, which helps too.

Defining idea...

'It had only one fault. It was kind of lousy.'

JAMES THURBER

How did it go?

Q None of the business plans I have seen mention manufacturing products. What use are these example plans to us?

A *Actually you can find many US examples of manufacturing plans – and remember, every business is unique and therefore there will be areas you need to add that aren't contained in any business plan you have seen, and likewise there will be areas of the plan above that simply do not need to be included. Other companies' business plans should only be used as a guide.*

A Is it better to lay out the business plan portrait or landscape?

Q *I have written business plans in both formats and personally prefer landscape if I am including lots of financial tables. It really is just a question of preference.*

Q I don't believe the market size and value estimates in the market surveys I am reading. I don't think they define the market in the same way as we do. How can I trust them?

A *This is a common problem. It depends on the type of business you are in, but could you conduct some market research of your own? Sometimes this can be done inexpensively through sampling, and may still be statistically valid. You are right to resist the temptation to base your plan on numbers you don't trust.*

22

Presenting your future

Everything you do and say regarding the business is being monitored. Whoever you talk to about your company should leave the conversation feeling positive about you and the business.

You may feel like a performing monkey at times, but it's a small price to pay for all those peanuts!

Software products such as PowerPoint are incredibly useful, but the art of presenting is more than knowing how to operate software and the space button on your laptop. To really wow clients and investors with a presentation using visual references or printed material (remember to keep the supporting material very brief) it is imperative that you talk more than show, otherwise the slides or sheets of paper will begin to blur in the mind of the observer and the exercise becomes pointless. Always go for the exciting facts and succinct points – no waffle or fluffy page filling. We can all see through the people who are presenting graphs rather than explaining facts. Good presentation is all about confidence in the material you are discussing and your ability to field queries and questions relating to the

Here's an idea for you...

Make a PowerPoint presentation of your business plan that contains no more than seven slides. This exercise will help you condense information and hopefully will become an early draft of the actual presentation that you will need to make in the future to potential investors or suppliers. Keep the information on the slides to a minimum. Practice talking through the presentation as many times as you can – each time you do your points will become stronger and clearer, and before long you will have memorised the perfect speech.

presentation. Never begin a presentation unsure what it is exactly you are going to say. Write your own presentation and don't rely on others to provide the data – you should understand it perfectly if you are the one who is likely to be grilled on the finer points.

If you are invited in to a bank, firm of accountants or the office of a potential investor to talk over your business plan, be sure to provide the documentation that you are intending to talk through well in advance of the meeting. As a rule you should be looking at ten days to two weeks ahead. This will allow people to read over the material in advance, and possibly prepare questions for you. This is much more effective than bringing the plan 'blind' to the meeting, since, not having read it through, they may not understand certain parts of your presentation. They will then have to read the documentation later on. This is not the way to get results!

Even if it is just a conceptual or temporary logo, the branding of your new enterprise needs to start from day one. The business plan should include your logo, and any cover letters or correspondence with potential suppliers, investors or customers should be printed on headed paper as soon as possible. Creating your company look not only makes you look far more professional, it also begins to build brand awareness for you and your business, even if that business is currently nothing more than a great idea and a couple of dog-eared pieces of paper.

For more about branding your business and creating a logo, check out IDEA 2, *Big, bold and a little bit cheeky.*

Try another idea...

A business is always bigger than just one person and with that rationale it is important to 'employ' as many people as possible in flying the flag and singing your praises. This is networking at its best. Whether they be relations or friends from the pub, talk about your business idea and get them talking about it. By constantly reminding others about what it is you are trying to achieve, all sorts of useful contacts will begin to make themselves apparent. If you are in the market for an accountant or a solicitor it will be recommendations from these sources that inevitably lead you on to finding the right business partners for your enterprise.

'Only a fool doesn't judge by appearances.'
OSCAR WILDE

Defining idea...

How did it go?

Q Our plan is still a little bit up in the air as we are still trying to finalise our pricing structure and gain competitor information. Should we wait a little longer before working on the presentation?

A *Start creating the slides just for the areas you have locked down, even if this is only your marketing strategy or plans for the website. The more you are thinking about presenting information about your business, the better your presentation will become. The rest will follow along later.*

Q We are planning on launching a design agency and want to use the opportunity of presenting the business to showcase some of our designs and previous portfolios – this will take the presentation to far longer than seven slides. Is this problematic?

A *Don't mix the presentation of the business plan with a pitch for new clients or a showcase of ability. By all means include an example or montage of design work, but really one presentation is required for the business and another to present work. Swamping your audience with too much information can be counter-productive.*

Q How many hours will it take to produce a PowerPoint presentation?

A *You get faster the more you do it, but even with all the information to hand it will probably take a day of fiddling with the visuals before you feel satisfied. Estimate that it will take the equivalent of twenty hours' work to produce a good job.*

23

The language of lords

The executive summary should always form the start of your business plan, but paradoxically it should always be the last part that you write.

What you are trying to achieve with an executive summary is similar to the back-cover blurb of a novel: get them hooked, don't just list all the fancy things you intend to buy and sell.

Once you have a first draft of your complete business plan it is time to start looking at creating the executive summary. You are looking to write no more than about three pages. A summary should be a brief précis of the main points in your business plan. It should not include any information that is not contained elsewhere in the plan. The purpose is to give readers a quick overview of the plan before they read it (or decide not to bother), so it must be an accurate reflection of the plan. The trick is to keep it as short and attractive as possible, because you are also, in effect, writing a teaser to entice your reader to continue reading. What is going to grab their attention? What is going to excite and have them thinking about you and your business and what, primarily, is going to hook them to read the full plan?

Here's an idea for you...

Show your executive summary to your accountant, bank manager and solicitor for candid feedback. Explain that this is a draft and you are looking for the areas that they find weak. You might be surprised how three different parties all make very similar comments. Don't ignore their comments. Rewrite the summary again and again until both they and you are happy with the final results.

SURPRISE, SURPRISE

The summary should not reveal all of your secrets and surprises – the business plan can still add to the reader's excitement. Use the executive summary to hint at surprises contained within. A good executive summary should be self-sufficient and not require any other supporting documents. It should be possible to read and digest it within a couple of minutes, otherwise it is wasted. Remember to use bullet points and headings to make it easy to read.

LAST MINUTE?

The executive summary, quite simply, could be your one opportunity to get the right investor, supplier or customer on board. Treat it with the same time and effort that is going into the rest of your business plan. If your reader does not engage with the executive summary then he is unlikely to read on, so come out with all guns blazing. If your executive summary takes just as long to write as the plan proper, this is no bad thing. Check it through again and again for errors and omissions and get someone else to proofread it too. Try reading it aloud; you'll be amazed at how different it seems, and you will probably find things that can be improved.

WHAT TO INCLUDE

Your summary should introduce the reader to:

- The business – name of the company, company particulars and branding.
- What it intends to achieve – description of the purpose, be it retail, manufacturing or tertiary, and an introduction to potential market share and financial projections.
- How it intends to achieve its goals – marketing, PR, growth strategy, operations and market analysis.
- Who is going to make sure it achieves – the management team and organisational structure.

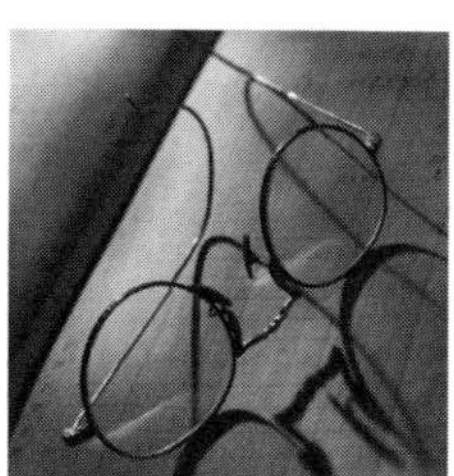

Try another idea...

The executive summary is worth nothing without the killer business plan that backs it up and explains the finer points in detail. To learn more, check out IDEA 21, *Magnum opus*.

Defining idea...

'Everyone is in business for himself, for he is selling his services, labor or ideas. Until one realizes that this is true, he will not take conscious charge of his life and will always be looking outside himself for guidance.'
SIDNEY MADWED, poet

How did it go?

Q I am reluctant to ask for comments from solicitors and accountants because it will just cost more. Can't I just get feedback from friends and family?

A *This is a valid point – you should try to keep professional fees down. Feedback from family and friends will not be sufficient, though. The best people to ask for an opinion are those who you intend to hit with the plan once it is complete. By involving them early in the proceedings you get the business known and you stroke a few egos along the way. You could also try people working in the same industry, but make sure that this will not alert the competition.*

Q Is it possible to squeeze an executive summary onto just one page?

A *Of course! Use the space that the summary needs and no more. If it hooks your reader to read the rest of the plan and gives them an instant overview and understanding of your business, then you have succeeded.*

Q I'm not sure how to make the summary 'sell' the plan. Do you have any tips?

A *Highlight the good news – for example, the projected turnover and profit level after three years, the return on capital, the time it will take for the business to pay back the investment and the long-term growth potential. Make sure that these figures are as accurate as you can make them, and that they are fully supported by evidence in the plan. Remember, most investors are thinking about what is in it for them – what percentage return are they going to make, and how long they will have to commit their investment funds for.*

24

Surviving due diligence

Undergoing 'due diligence' can be a horrific experience if you are unprepared, but with the right preparation it can go smoothly with minimal disruption.

Due diligence is not unlike having your underwear drawer on show to the world; you wouldn't mind that much, but one of the team seems to want to sniff your pants!

'Due diligence' is usually carried out on a company when an investor or another company is seriously interested in investing in or merging with your business. They need to be sure that all of the claims they have read in the business plan, seen in presentations and the answers they have received to their queries over the past weeks or months are actually true. It is a form of protection for them but can be a harrowing experience for you. If your claims are true, it should mean that you are now very close to receiving the investment and assistance that you require.

Here's an idea for you...

Have every member of staff document procedures so that they are on record. This is never a waste of time; the procedure documents can form the basis of a training pack and this process ensures that no member of staff is indispensable.

Consultants are sent in to 'dig' within the business. They are primarily there to ascertain the value of the business and its ability to meet the requirements set by you and the investors or potential joint venture partners. Senior staff will be quizzed relentlessly about every single aspect of the business. A good consultant will also make it his or her job to find out the 'truth' from other members of staff. They are not looking to catch you out, but to ensure that the business objectives are understood from the top down. Casual conversations with junior or part-time staff can reveal an awful lot about the true working practices and morale of the staff.

The reality of the situation is that every number, claim, projection and line entry you have ever committed to paper of computer file will be scrutinised and absolutely nothing will be taken as fact unless there is some supporting evidence.

HOW TO PREPARE FOR THE ONSLAUGHT

It is imperative that you file, back-up and can put your hands on absolutely everything, especially financial records, no matter how old. There can be no excuses as to why documents are missing, corrupt or only partially complete. Organise your files before the assessors arrive, not when they are in the building. You will only be asked for the information, and, as the people sent in will probably be charging by the hour or by the day (and you will foot the bill), it is in your financial interest to ensure that documentation can be found quickly and easily. Don't forget that it will help in the assessors' report if they comment on how professional and organised the company is. Treat your assessors with respect, but don't grovel. They are paid professionals doing a job and they should be left in peace to do it. As you are paying, you want value for money no matter how antagonistic some of the questioning might be.

Try another idea...

The due diligence procedure will not stop at questioning the previous or current successes of the business. You will also be asked to elaborate on past mistakes and failures and what you have done to address these failings. To learn more, check out IDEA 29, *Action/reaction.*

The assessors will speak not only with you. No matter what your reasons are for 'protecting' other members of staff from being grilled, they will be asked some delving questions and if you appear to be interfering with their answers, you will be asked to leave. Ensure that all of the staff are briefed well in advance if you can – you are all on show and if your staff aren't prepared, or don't take the procedure seriously, it can and will have a detrimental effect on the assessor's report.

It may seem a bit odd, given that the reason you have probably approached a large investor is to raise funds, that due diligence costs you a significant amount of money, but it does. More often than not, especially if you are dealing with venture capital firms, the cost associated with sending in a team of chartered accountants is met by you, on the understanding that if the investment goes ahead that money will come back. The only problem is that if the deal falls through, for whatever reason, you are left with a huge bill.

Defining idea...

'Economists are people who work with numbers but who don't have the personality to be accountants.'
ANONYMOUS

How did it go?

Q The customer services manager says that the current system is really straightforward and therefore doesn't need to be documented. How can I persuade her to do it?

A *You must insist that she does it anyway. It might be straightforward, but if she were to leave the company, would her replacement know where to pick up? Make sure that there is a procedure document, and test it yourself by working through the points and ensuring that you too could walk into the role if need be.*

Q I run a very small consultancy firm on my own. What is there to document?

A *Everything! You need to outline how orders or tenders are found, how the potential customer is contacted, how the pricing is agreed, how that figure was reached and make a record of the consultancy's past jobs – just for starters.*

Q This is going to take forever! Do you want me to spend three weeks doing this instead of making money?

A *This is the perennial problem for one-man bands; there never seems to be enough time to do paperwork. Documenting procedures, however, helps to turn your business into a saleable commodity for investors – so think of it as adding value to your business. Take your time; you don't have to do all the work at once, and it certainly shouldn't take three weeks to complete.*

THAMESDOWN WELFARE RIGHTS FORUM
CYMDEITHAS TAI CYMDOGA
NEIGHBOURHOOD HOUSING ASS

25

Know thyself

Self-assessment is hard. Either we are unfair on ourselves and are unwilling to give ourselves credit or we blow our own horn a bit too much. It's time for some objectivity.

Be fair to yourself and to others when assessing individual worth; if you get it wrong, your colleagues are likely to become extremely upset.

You might regard yourself as ideal for your role and ideal for running your own business, and you may well be right, but it is always worthwhile treating yourself (just for a few minutes) as a stranger. If you met yourself, how would you describe that meeting? If your answers include loving, adorable, and a great guy, you're probably not taking the exercise particularly seriously. Understanding what skills you hold, and more importantly, what your weaknesses are, will quickly determine what skill sets the business needs to employ to make the venture a success. Do not ignore the fact that you are not particularly strong at certain aspects of running a business – not everyone is an effective communicator, or negotiator, or happy to sit typing invoices. To pretend to yourself and others that you can do absolutely everything required by the business is foolhardy.

Here's an idea for you...

Write out, in full, the job description when you are recruiting. Now write down the core competencies of that role in two sections, 'need to have' and 'nice to have'. By explaining your requirements, your vacancy will not only be more attractive to the people best-suited for the job, but will minimise the number of no-hopers applying for the role.

DIRECTORS WITHOUT PORTFOLIOS

A very clever way to make your business appear successful and well organised, along with filling any gaps in your and the other directors' skill sets, is to organise a skills audit. This exercise determines what skills are held within the company and exposes any gaps or weaknesses. Ask everyone to list their own skills, giving details, and identifying areas of weakness. Explain that honesty is essential, and that the information will not be held against them – it is simply to help the company discover what skills it has and what it lacks.

The answer to these shortfalls is to find non-executive directors or less-formal business partners from outside of the business to act in the company's best interest. It is often the case that directors of a business all come from a similar background or industry. In many ways this is ideal – you have a number of individuals who are all very experienced in the trade that the company is intending to offer. Having said that, if all your staff have similar backgrounds, you will find that skills overlap and there remain some gaps – more often than not in the Finance Department, unless you all happen to be accountants setting up a new venture. It is wise to secure the assistance of someone prepared to act as a director of finance. You will quickly find that those persons looking after the cash of a business will identify all the projects that sound wonderful but will eventually turn out to be unprofitable. A good director of finance will save you a fortune.

Try another idea...

Knowing your staff's strengths is half the battle, but if that winning attitude is kept secret, or is not conveyed well to others, it is going to be difficult to succeed. To learn more, check out IDEA 13, *What you think all the guns is for?*

CHOOSING YOUR FRIENDS

Assessing the skills of others does not stop at the recruitment and employment of the directors of the business; it must carry right down to the rank and file of the business and be foremost in your mind when you are hiring staff. Always prepare well for interviews and be absolutely clear in your mind what you are looking for in each candidate. If the role you are looking to fill requires a good working knowledge of computers and specific software packages, do not be tempted to hire someone who promises to learn – find the candidate who fits the vacancy, do not alter the role to fit the candidate.

Defining idea...

'If you're going to be a healer, it's not enough to read books and learn allegorical stories. You need to get your feet wet, get some clinical experience under your belt.'
DIANE FROLOY and ANDREW SCHNEIDER, screenwriters

How did it go?

Q I am not planning on taking on a member of staff until the business is eighteen months old and financially established. Can't this exercise wait?

A *If you are planning to take on a member of staff, ever, then create the job description now, when your mind is still full of ideas from writing the business plan and discussing the business every hour of every day. You will be in a stronger position to write the description now. It can always be finalised nearer the time.*

Q What is the significance of the 'nice to haves'?

A *Hopefully, when the job is advertised you will attract only suitable candidates. Having a number of 'nice to haves' will allow you to choose 'a first among equals' because they will have not only satisfied the core competencies but also bring extra skills or experience (or a very attractive list of contacts) to the role.*

Q I'm having trouble getting people to assess their own skills. What should I do?

A *Try doing it in group sessions, using a white board. Explain what is needed, and then write down your own skills and shortcomings on the board. Depending on the group, you can then ask everyone to complete their own assessment on paper while you wait, or you can laboriously drag the information out of each person and write it on the whiteboard – this may take more time, but may be necessary if the individuals are not used to this kind of work. Make sure someone keeps a record, though!*

26

Selling out before you have begun

There are times when you can't do it alone and another individual must be brought in to make your business happen. This is not necessarily a bad thing if you know what you're looking for.

Yes, you're selling out, but what is better: making your business a success or proving that you like banging your head against a wall?

While many of us would like to handle every aspect of the business and retain complete control, sometimes we have to compromise to get the project off the ground. If you, like most new businesses, require funding to start the ball rolling, there is often more sympathy and respect given from banks and other lenders if you have already convinced another party to help share the risk and invest some of their own capital into the venture. Taking on a business partner is a massive decision, whether they are a friend, a family member or an outsider. The important thing

Here's an idea for you...

Create and send a proposal to an organisation you have identified as a potential joint venture partner. Don't contact a competitor at this stage, but if there is a firm working in a related business, contact them and see if they bite. While your plan may have been to build up gradually, a powerful joint venture could see you catapulted from new business to major player.

from your perspective is to take on the right partner and to make it explicitly clear to both sides what each expects of the other. The ideal scenario is that your partner will not only double your seed capital but will take on half the workload. It doesn't always work as neatly as this, but it's an ideal to strive for.

An alternative to involving an individual in the risk and workload associated with launching a new business is to approach existing businesses and enter the sometime bizarre, sometimes scary, but often lucrative world of joint ventures. This option simply isn't available in some industries, but if you're planning an internet component to your business, there is a good chance, assuming you do your research, of attracting a strong established partner to help you get off the ground. As with accepting financial help from an angel or venture capitalist, no one enters a joint venture out of sheer benevolence – they do it to increase their own profit or market share over a certain period of time. The overriding advantage of entering into a joint venture with an established organisation is the knock-on benefits you receive in addition to the cash: sharing advertising and marketing, facilities, staff and advice and assistance from personnel you couldn't possibly afford to consult or retain.

When you take on a business partner or enter into a joint venture with another firm, there is a 'penalty' – you will have to give them a share of the business. In return for their assistance, partners are looking for a share in your future success and this is often taken in the form of shares in the company. Once your business becomes profitable these shareholders will be looking for dividends (and healthy ones at that) that will hopefully pay back their original investment many times over. Many people looking to start businesses are very reluctant to grant any part of the company over to another individual, but the question remains, are you able to start the business and give it a fighting chance without their assistance? If the answer is no, then you need to bite the bullet.

Try another idea...

If you are looking for alternative ways to raise funding for your business, check out IDEA 15, *The Tet offensive.*

The reality is that it is very hard to run a profitable business. Inexperienced people often think that it is a sign of weakness to give up any share of the profit, but if you don't, in many cases you will find that you don't make any profit at all. A bird in the hand is definitely worth two in the bush!

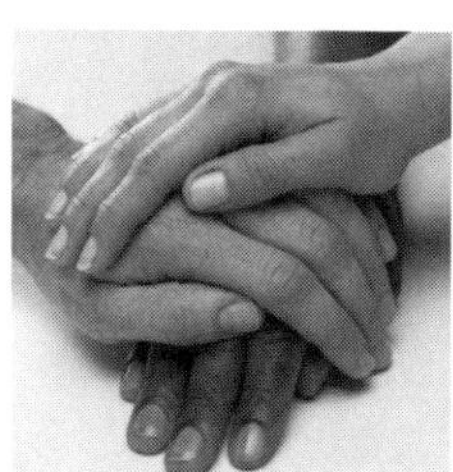

Defining idea...

'A good listener is not only popular everywhere, but after a while he gets to know something.'

WILSON MIZNER, US screenwriter

How did it go?

Q Surely to entice a joint venture partner we would have to reveal an awful lot about how we plan to operate? This information could be passed on to our competitors. What can we do to protect ourselves?

A *You will have to reveal pretty much everything about your plans, state of finances, ambitions and reasons for contacting the firm, but equally they will have to do the same if the joint venture is to become a serious possibility. Your introductory letter need not be too detailed; if they agree to meet, it would be in everyone's interest if you provide a non-disclosure agreement (NDA) before the meeting takes place.*

Q I have an interested party who is both qualified to help run the business and prepared to contribute to the seed capital of the business. She wants 50% of the business if the partnership is to go ahead. Is this fair?

A *Assuming that you have exhausted all other channels, you must look at what is best for the business over the long term and not what is best for you right now. It's all very well to own 100% of a business, but if that business is worth nothing, or is highly likely to fail in its first eighteen months from lack of investment, then the whole venture is pointless. Better to own 50% of something than 100% of nothing!*

27

You're nothing!

When you are constructing your business plan and when you are actually operating the business, you should always watch what your competition is doing. Imitate their successes and avoid their mistakes.

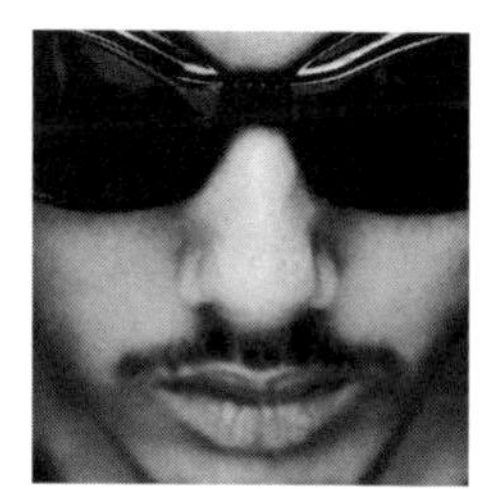

You don't have to wear a balaclava and spend your evenings suspended above buildings trying to break into a competitor's office – although this could be a lot of fun… There are easier ways!

Sun Tzu teaches that if you study the enemy intimately, you will win the war. Waging war and competing in the commercial market are not dissimilar. Although you are unlikely to lose your head if you fail, it is much better to be the winner and have your enemies begging for mercy at your feet – or at least conceding some of their market share. A simple way to monitor your competition is to test their service as much as you can – have members of your staff phone them up, order

Here's an idea for you...

If you use sequential numbering on your invoices/receipts – stop! Have this altered immediately; someone out there is monitoring your business. Place some orders with competitors and see how they number documents. This intelligence is frightening, both in terms of what you can learn about your competition and how easy it is to obtain.

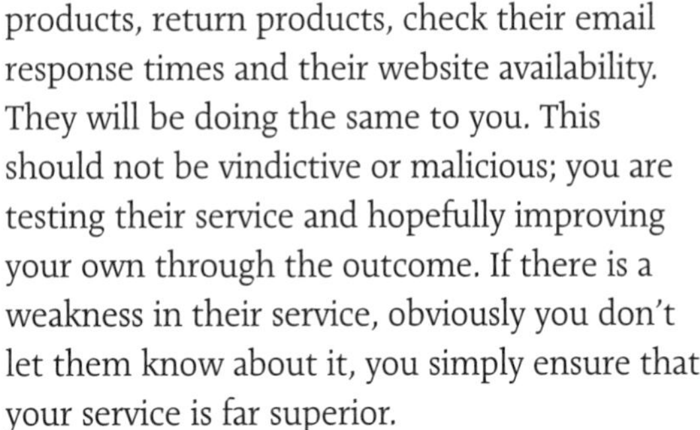

products, return products, check their email response times and their website availability. They will be doing the same to you. This should not be vindictive or malicious; you are testing their service and hopefully improving your own through the outcome. If there is a weakness in their service, obviously you don't let them know about it, you simply ensure that your service is far superior.

Never give away your position and strengths but know their weaknesses – use the trade press to keep abreast of competitors' machinations. Who are they doing deals with? How are they advertising? From adverts alone you should be able to make an educated guess about how much is being spent on marketing. Does your competition run any promotions with clients? If so, get the details of the deal and explore, as best you can, where their products/services are selling and to whom.

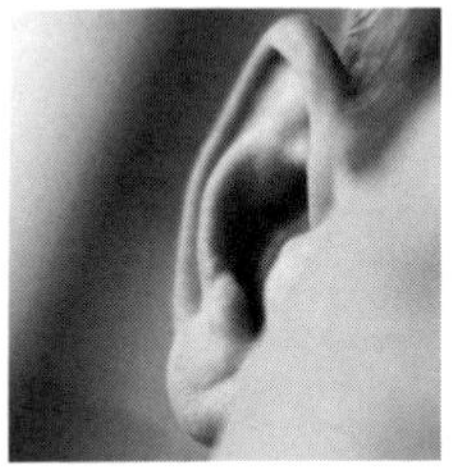

It is reasonably straightforward to monitor their staff retention through how many adverts they are placing for staff vacancies. Note that to disguise growth, some companies advertise for a temporary position due to maternity leave – or even paternity leave now. This can be a very clever way to both bring candidates in on a short-term contract and, if they are suitable, make their contract more long term, thus protecting the company from having to retain unsuitable staff and hiding the number of new employees from competitors' eyes.

Try another idea...

Watching your competition is a sure way to improve your offering, but your own customers and clients can be a fountain of knowledge in this area too. Ask and ye shall receive. To learn more, check out IDEA 48, *What are you crying about?*

When I was with Amazon I was given a budget every week to buy books on the internet from our competitors. Why? Well, I would like to believe that Amazon were incredibly benevolent employers and they knew how to retain a bibliophile; however, the reason was much more clever, and nothing to do with me at all. Every Monday at 11.00 a.m. I would place an order with five competitors and over the week the orders would arrive. On each of the shipping notes/invoices there was a shipping number or reference – and all of these companies were using sequential numbering. So, for the cost of a few orders, we were able to see how many orders the company had shipped ever, calculate an approximate value of their entire business and see the number of orders they received a week – priceless.

Defining idea...

'All you need in this life is ignorance and confidence; then success is sure.'
MARK TWAIN

How did it go?

Q It looks as if our competitors have got wise and decided to adopt coded shipping numbers. Finance wonders how useful this exercise would be for us – are there other ways to see what they are up to?

A Even if you are unable to determine your competitors' sales figures, you can still mark them on other points. As well as monitoring their ability to confirm orders and despatch, follow up on any customer service queries you may have and, if you return the products, how good is their service?

Q Will ordering from competitors tell us anything else?

A You will also be able to see what, if any, marketing deals have been struck with third parties. Are there any flyers contained in your delivery that advertise banks or credit cards? Where else are your competitors earning revenue and can you do the same? Another excellent method is to employ people who have worked for your competitors – they will be able to tell you an awful lot about the personalities and processes involved. Sales and marketing people are especially useful for this, since they are at the hard end of the business and tend to be competitive types. Now they're working for you, they'll probably want to beat their old company.

28

Having peripheral vision

Variety is the spice of life. From the moment you start creating your business plan you should be exploring every possible way that the business can make money.

This isn't about having fingers in every pie and getting in a mess. It's to ensure that you are maximising profit for you and your business.

Although the strongest business planning revolves around a business's core values, shrewd entrepreneurs do not put all of their eggs into one basket. It may be that you look at adding a website or a mail order capacity to your business plan as a way to seem like a multi-channel, 'with-it' sort of business. Or you may include the other sales channels as serious money earners but not be truly committed to them, by not allowing enough for staff recruitment and development. But these simple activities could prove, sometimes very quickly, to be your main strengths and they must be planned from the outset. Despite your confidence in your retail outlet selling *x* number of chess sets per week, it could be that you really don't have the footfall (passing custom) to support the business. Your website, designed and built

Here's an idea for you...

If you are planning to operate a retail or catering business, produce flyers or mini-catalogues showcasing a selection of products or promotions. Now negotiate an insert into the next edition of the local free paper. If you promote the business address, phone number or web address (or a combination of all three), it will quickly show whether there is a potential market for a mail order business or, in the catering arena, home-delivery and large group bookings. This could open up a number of new sales channels for your business.

Defining idea...

'Be wary of the man who urges an action in which he himself incurs no risk.'
JOAQUIN SETANTI, philosopher

for a few hundred pounds at the insistence of your nephew, could turn out to be the resounding success story of the company if sales exceed expectations. Don't sell yourself, or your sales channels, short. If you are planning to have multiple routes to market, plan each of them with as much care and attention as your main business objective.

STAFF SKILLS

Treat your own skills and the skills of your staff with a completely mercenary approach. If you or a staff member is a skilled writer, farm out your talents to other companies – by using the infrastructure of your business to pitch for work, you can charge a far healthier fee for the work and justify a split in revenues between the author and the business.

Is your business such that you could spare a staff member one afternoon a week to talk or present at tradeshows or to other organisations? Again, using the resources of the business to promote these talents means a larger fee for all involved.

There are so many ways to earn extra cash by selling your staff's skills to other businesses; remind them that although they might earn more by freelancing full-time, it could take them several years before they developed enough contacts to get a steady flow of work. By working for you in this way, they increase their income at no risk.

Try another idea...

Finding suitable property in which to operate your business can be a minefield. To learn more, check out IDEA 7, *That's so 'des res'*.

THE SPACE AROUND YOU

When buying or leasing premises there is often a price point that, once breached, means for very little extra cost you can acquire a tremendous amount of extra space. If the space is surplus to requirements, sub-let part of the building to another individual or organisation at a competitive rate. Proportionately you will be recouping a large amount of rental income whilst only sacrificing a small amount of space. But watch out – if all your small tenants go broke in a recession, you'll end up having to pay the entire rent. This can and does happen, so be careful with your selection of tenants and the agreements you make with them. Often retail premises are easier to let than offices during hard times; it matters less if you lose a tenant when there are others eager to take their place.

Defining idea...

'If we don't succeed, we run the risk of failure.'
DAN QUAYLE

How did it go?

Q We have some staff who are great at promotion. How can we sell their services to others?

A *Often you can get good contacts at tradeshows, even with firms you already know. If they see your people in action and are impressed, why not offer a marketing/promotional package for their next show?*

Q Our business is really strapped for cash and this promotion would constitute a major portion of our marketing spend. Isn't it a bit risky?

A *At some stage you are probably going to place an advert in the local paper anyway. Adverts are not cheap and a quarter page in a local rag can be surprisingly expensive. An insert is often more effective, and if you retain 1,000 to be handed out as flyers, you will be enjoying two separate promotions for the price of one.*

Q We feel flyers are a bit tacky. Won't this promotion give customers the wrong impression?

A *Flyers don't have to be the standard look and feel – there are a number of innovative options such as embossed, credit card sized, seasonally themed and gatefold. Good artwork and good paper make great flyers.*

29

Action/reaction

When starting a business you must expect setbacks; no one gets it completely right first time, ever. The secret of success is in how you react to a problem.

Running away from the first surprise bill or delay to a schedule is not a good reaction – it's pretty hard to run when you're committed, and it solves nothing.

GOOD TIMES

When everything is going to plan and life couldn't get any better, you are right to congratulate yourself for forward planning and great organisational skills, but the danger can be that you become too complacent and cocky. Success comes from maintaining focus on the job at hand. Be sure to remind yourself that each week, each month and each quarter can bring with them a whole new set of obstacles and hurdles to thwart your plans of world domination and a yacht populated only by bronzed beauties.

Most problems facing businesses amount to cash flow problems. When times are good and things are going swimmingly, it really is prudent to put away money for

Here's an idea for you...

Keep a collection of articles from the national, international and local press showing businesses that are failing or have gone under. The press is excellent at providing all the details those businesses would rather you did not know – from multi-national scandals involving the 'accidental' shredding of important financial data to internal rivalry and twisted love triangles. Make yourself aware of all the potential pitfalls right from the start and be sure to avoid them.

Defining idea...

'Finance is the art of passing currency from hand to hand until it finally disappears.'
ROBERT W. SARNOFF, US media mogul

the rainy day that could be waiting for you just around the corner. Holding back on spending every penny available to you will not arrest your development as a business, because, lets face it, if you can continue to exceed your targets every month soon the kitty will be big enough for a rainy season, not just a day. What's better than giving yourself a good pay rise for all that hard effort?

BAD TIMES

Any setbacks in the early days of creating and launching a business can hit those involved really hard. You're doing your best, you have invested time, money and effort into getting the project off the ground and somebody, somewhere, isn't signing the lease you need for the building, or setting you up with a credit card machine in time for your launch. These are trying times indeed and although it might make you feel better (temporarily) if you shout and rage about it, it will not make the situation any better. Learn from setbacks as you do from successes. If things just take longer than they should to organise and arrange, adjust all future date-specific estimates to allow for these unforeseen delays.

Making your mistakes early on in the firm's life is much more beneficial than if you do this many years down the line. When you are new, you are less likely to have your mistakes reported in the press, and though the values involved if the mistakes are cash flow related might well be significant at the time, there are usually ways to fix the problem. And most importantly, if you learn from the mistakes you are less likely to repeat the episode again.

Setbacks can remain par for the course for all the years you remain in business. To learn more, check out IDEA 51, *The Poseidon adventure.*

Try another idea...

Controlling cash flow really is the secret of business survival. Psychologically, it is always easier to spend than to save, and companies do this just as much as individuals. That means all your suppliers, customers and competitors are doing it – and you are the one who will get squeezed if you are not alert. Try to institute systems to ensure that it's the other firm who takes the cash flow strain in any arrangement – for example, contracts with penalty clauses, deals where the other party pays for bank charges and cash-only terms for most customers help to keep the pressure off.

How did it go?

Q I have tried to collect stories of business problems as you suggest, but the ones I have found all refer to enormous corporations losing millions and billions. My business plans to turn over 200,000 p.a. How can we make a comparison?

A *Ignore the values involved and look to see what went wrong. If a director was greedy and pocketed 24 million, the same could happen to you from a manager dipping into the petty cash every week (but stealing a bit less than*

24 million, probably). Often large corporations go bust because they take unnecessary risks, like investing in a developing country with a poor legal system and a corrupt government, or using financial instruments they don't fully understand. The same is true for small firms; things go wrong when you are careless or overconfident.

Q None of the articles seem to mention companies in our industry. Where's the relevance?

A Business is business, and whether you are selling bananas or hedge funds, they all fail for similar reasons.

Q Is there any sure way to avoid cash flow problems?

A In most businesses they will arise from time to time. The trick is to anticipate them before they occur – your bank will love you if you inform them that you need a temporary loan before *the crisis hits, because it shows you are acting responsibly. Many problems can be avoided during the negotiation of the initial deal; once you're committed, it is harder to cope with unforeseen cash flow problems. Try to get good lines of credit from your bank and elsewhere, and when you are expanding, be especially careful. Many businesses go broke from 'overtrading', which generally means selling too many things on credit and running out of cash.*

30

Being all ears

With any new idea, we naturally want to do as much as we can on our own, but being too proud can lead to disaster. Look for others who offer good advice for free; if you don't, your competition certainly will.

Look to experienced business development organisations for advice, and read serious technical books about corporate finance and investment decisions. Business is one area where theory really does turn out to be applicable in practice.

LETTING GO

There should be an element of secrecy involved in setting up a new business. The fewer the people who know the finer details, the more likely that your idea will not be hijacked by another individual or company. But you also need to build awareness of your business right from day one. You will not divulge sensitive information to

Here's an idea for you...

Make a point of contacting at least one organisation in your local area and setting up a meeting to determine how useful they could be in helping your business achieve its goals. During your half hour chat you will probably be given sound advice *and* the contact details of individuals or organisations who will also help you move the business forward.

random members of the public, you will be entering into discussions with professionals who are either paid or volunteer to offer advice to businesses. There is an important difference between the two!

WHAT'S ON OFFER?

Depending on where you are and the nature of the business you are planning to launch, you may be able to obtain anything from a cash grant, tax breaks and access to qualified staff to financial advice and moral support. It is your responsibility, as the person driving the business, to research every option and, if possible, meet as many potential helping hands as you can.

FROM WHOM?

A search on the internet is your best place to start. Very quickly you will begin to appreciate the myriad organisations out there that exist solely to support businesses. Some are for profit and some offer their services gratis. What you pay for may not necessarily be more valuable to you than what is given for free. In the UK, a few searches to start you on your way should include 'business link' 'DTI' 'Chamber of Commerce' 'British Embassy [name of country you are planning to trade in]' 'British Council' 'Business Learning & Skills' and your local government website.

WHY?

So much of setting up a new business comes with a price. It may feel strange that individuals or organisations are prepared to be so benevolent – but remember they receive funding from somewhere (usually from the government through taxation) and therefore in a roundabout way you have been paying for this assistance for years; you'd be crazy not to 'cash in' now. We can also become a little blinkered about our own abilities. Whilst it is good to be confident and passionate about a new business, involving a third-party can mean even more good ideas are thrown into the mix. Why not give your business an even greater chance of success?

Try another idea...

As well as turning to others for advice you will probably have a track record of enjoying success and failure in your own right. It is equally important to tap into your own memory to avoid similar mistakes reoccurring. To learn more, check out IDEA 29, *Action/reaction.*

Defining idea...

'Good advice is something a man gives when he is too old to set a bad example.'

FRANÇOIS DE LA ROCHEFOUCAULD

How did it go?

Q I wasn't very comfortable in the meeting because the person I met insisted on taking notes. Could all of my research and planning get into a rival's hands?

A *This is unlikely. Note-taking usually means that the person you met was interested in what you had to say. The chances are that you will receive a follow-up call in a few days offering you even more advice and a few extra contacts.*

Q The person I am due to meet has already told me they have no retail experience; what's the point?

A *In some ways business is just business; although they have no experience in your industry, they will be familiar with what all businesses need when starting up – namely, a solid plan and good cash-flow management. Meet them and then decide.*

Q I find that a lot of government agencies that are supposed to help businesses are useless. Can the DTI really help me?

A *When was the last time you dealt with these bodies? You may well find that a lot has changed.*

31

Calamity Jane

When every penny counts it may seem strange to leave a large percentage of your working capital aside for a rainy day, but that's what you need to do.

Be too cautious of course and the business won't have a fighting chance of succeeding at all – tiptoe rather than crawl.

Any monies borrowed, if at all possible, must be secured on some of your assets, even if the lender is not asking for such a provision. Yes, you could declare yourself bankrupt if it all went terribly wrong, but if you truly believe in the business that you are creating, you should never get into the position of having to declare yourself bankrupt – if you are paying enough attention to essentials such as your cash flow, you'll see the downward spiral before or whilst it is happening and react accordingly instead of reacting after the event.

There are times when the risk of launching a business involves you putting absolutely everything on the line, including your car, house, kids, family pet and every last penny of savings. This is unwise. If the idea is that good, there are other

Here's an idea for you...

Take some time to scan the jobs in the national press and look for the skills and experience required for the roles you would be interested in applying for were you in the market. Is there something that you could be doing now (training through the business, for example) to ensure that you improve your marketable skills?

areas of investment open to you. Although you will be well regarded for showing such commitment, especially by banks, they won't be there to applaud if it all goes wrong – in fact, they will probably be the ones repossessing your vehicle and house. Avoid this at all costs.

As the months become years and you are able to say that you run an established business, don't lose sight of the ever-changing market. When creating your business plan, a lot of time and effort probably went into researching the market into which you were entering and the competition as it stood then. Over a period of months and years the market alters; consumers change allegiance and react differently to pricing models depending on what else is going on in terms of interest rates

Defining idea...

'First weigh the considerations, then take the risks.'

HELMUTH VON MOLTKE, German army general

and earnings. Competitors consolidate their position and sometimes fold. All this jostling around alters the picture at any given time. Keeping a keen eye on the industry should be an ongoing concern for everyone in the business. Something you would rather not think about, but nonetheless a very valid exercise, is to imagine the worst-case scenario. If, for whatever reason, the business is gone, you may be back in the job market looking to keep a roof over your head and your family fed. How would you do it?

Try another idea...

Despite all the best planning, sometimes things do go wrong, and the question is now how to make the situation right. To learn more, check out IDEA 51, *The Poseidon adventure.*

Defining idea...

'Take calculated risks. That is quite different from being rash.'

GEORGE S. PATTON, US army general

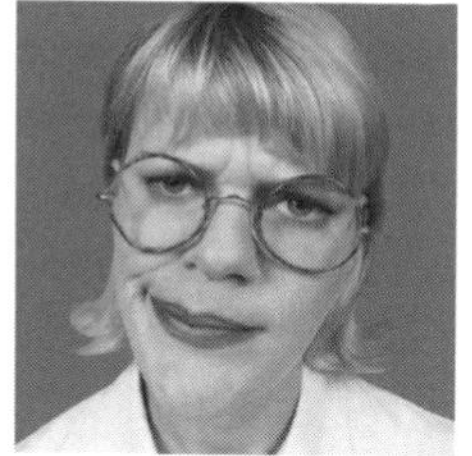

How did it go?

Q As I am now managing director, I don't think I would have any trouble re-entering the job market in a few years' time. Surely this exercise doesn't apply to me?

A *For the cost of incorporating a company (about £350 in the UK), anyone over 18 can become a managing director. At one stage I was managing director of three companies at the same time, but it doesn't really mean much – it is just a title. Potential future employers are going to be interested in what you have done and what you bring to their organisation, not what job title you gave yourself. In business you meet a lot of silly people who like to appear important; to the experienced eye, they are very obvious. Don't be one of them.*

Q We can't really afford training. Is there a cheaper way of doing it?

A *Certainly. Always look first at exchanging skills within the business. There is no reason why every member of the management team shouldn't be shown how to use the company accountancy software. Not only does this improve skills and knowledge, but it will be less of a problem if the bookkeeper is ill or leaves the business.*

32

Peter paying Paul

In an ideal world your customers would pay you before you had to pay your suppliers, but it rarely works that way. To stay afloat, you need to manage your cash flow.

In the majority of businesses, the pressure is on you to spend before you get paid. Effective cash flow is about ensuring that you have more money coming in than you have going out.

For sales to take place you will need to order products and materials, supply them to the customer, invoice them and, in many cases, wait to be paid. For this you will need a trading platform (a shop, office or website) and staff, which all costs money.

So how does it really work? You order the materials and services you need and sell them on to your customer, but it is the terms you have arranged with both that will determine your cash flow. Good cash flow management enhances profitability and is a key element in ensuring that your business survives.

Here's an idea for you...

Try to tighten the credit you offer to customers. For retail businesses, most payments are instantaneous, but there is still the option to take deposits for stock you haven't even ordered. For commercial businesses, drop your terms to 7 or 14 days rather than the standard 30 days – it's amazing how many companies will pay up without causing a fuss.

Your mission, quite simply, is to try and use other people's money to cover your expenditure. If you can manage this you will be cash rich and in a very healthy position. If at all possible, obtain immediate payment from your customers before providing the product or service. If, at the same time, you can pay your suppliers over a longer period – usually 30, but sometimes 60 or 90 days – you will have a very healthy cash flow. Crack this and maybe retirement and the front cover of *Time Magazine* are not so far away.

On occasion, it is possible to spread your banking custom and thus your ability to borrow more. By setting up separate accounts to handle each of your routes to market, such as internet sales, mail order sales or international sales, there is the possibility of creating multiple relationships with banks that will allow more access to lending and credit. As long as the business is not overstretched, and the loans are overdrafts that can be covered by the revenues from each of the sales channels, you are not breaking rules, just giving your business more options.

Defining idea...

'It is better to have a permanent income than to be fascinating.'
OSCAR WILDE

By definition, a new business has no track record and no sympathy from the firms it deals with. Even if you are bringing years of personal experience to the party, the sad truth is that when it comes to paying bills you will be hit the hardest in your first year. Suppliers may demand that your first order is paid for pro-forma (in advance). The bank may be reluctant to grant the overdraft facility you require. Much, if not all, of the business machinery must be purchased and you will pay deposits on your premises, hire-purchase items and other leases. In short, your first twelve months will be expensive, but you need them to be cheap until you get your income up. The net result is that you may need to earn much more in your first year than in subsequent years just to break even. Budget for being taken to the cleaners in your first year; the business world, it seems, is geared up for making the life of a start-up as hard as possible. The trick is to make it through to the other side and start earning more than you spend. You must make the difficult journey to the fabled world of profitability!

Try another idea...

It is important to account for cash flow right from the early days of planning your business. Understanding the rules of cash flow will alter the appearance of your projections. To learn more, check out IDEA 6, *Cheap at twice the price.*

It's time to put your negotiating powers to the test and try and get the most favourable terms for your business. Although you will have trouble convincing your suppliers in your first year to give you any special dispensation over and above their standard terms, there is no harm in asking. Whatever their terms are, be sure to pay up on time; if you don't, you are asking for trouble.

Defining idea...

'When a man tells you that he got rich through hard work, ask him: "Whose?"'

DON MARQUIS, author

How did it go?

Q Given how unfairly our suppliers treat us, we feel it is wrong to pressure our customers into paying faster than 30 days. Are we right?

A *Leave your benevolent tendencies at home! This is business, and ensuring your cash flow is positive is more important than worrying about another company or individual. By all means, if the company complains then revert to 30 days to keep relations amicable, but otherwise enjoy spending their money on more stock or your salary.*

Q One of our suppliers has offered better terms but we lose the 5% early-payer discount. Should we take the deal?

A *Probably not, unless you can swallow the extra cost in your margins. You really want the cheapest price possible and if that means paying after 30 days rather 60, then so be it. However, is that 5% a 'real' discount, or are there other suppliers whose normal price is 5% less? Be a miser, and take pains to reduce your cost of supply as much as you can without compromising on quality. If prices are high in the UK, have you tried buying what you need in China, Indonesia or Taiwan? You could be amazed at the money you save.*

33

Thinking macro

There is a chance that your business could become a huge success. Are you prepared physically and mentally to handle it? What would you do if things took off?

Many guides to starting and running businesses emphasise caution and safety. For the most part this is sound advice, but it is also wise to think about how to handle a big increase in business.

Don't start the celebrations yet – there is a lot to be done in the mean time! Although it may seem absurd to provide financial projections for the next three years when not a single day's trading has taken place, three years is not actually that far away. In fact, by the time the business is up and running, your days quickly turn into weeks and then, before you've come up for air, you are preparing your first year's accounts. So planning, or at least being aware that the years are passing, is a very sound way to conduct your projections. Ideally you should look for growth within the business but you are also looking to consolidate your position by this stage. Although increasing your market share will be a priority, and there will be a

Here's an idea for you...

Take your business projection further and rework your employment, variable and fixed costs to reflect how your expenditure would be affected by a spurt of growth. The numbers might seem staggering but you will see how you would cope and the amount that your business *could* be turning over in a matter of 36 months.

very significant cost associated with this, if you bought well in the first place, your initial setup costs – business machinery and premises – should still be earning their way and providing a return on that initial investment.

Sometimes fantastic luck and being in the right place at the right time turns what would have been a reasonably successful business into a runaway hit. New businesses can sometimes touch customers in such a refreshing way that they can't remember what they did before the business came along. Tapping into the Zeitgeist can just happen. It can be assisted if you are constantly thinking what people might need in about three years' time. Let your mind work overtime and try to work out all the possibilities.

Everyone warns you to prepare for the future, in case things don't go as well as planned. Tying yourself to long leases on plant and buildings can be dangerous. But another argument is that you should not to tie yourself in for too long in case things really take off. If you suddenly find that you require additional space, you should be able to up and leave and lease a much larger building. This will be a lot cheaper than having to pay rent on a number of separate properties, not to mention the problems associated with multiple locations, such as communication difficulties and a 'them-and-us' mentality forming among the staff.

Defining idea...

'There are no secrets to success. It is the result of preparation, hard work, and learning from failure.'
COLIN POWELL

It is also advisable to use your crystal ball and try to see beyond the town or city where you are currently based. Although you may well have decided upon your current location to minimise costs and reduce commuting for you and your staff, you may outgrow your current environs and have to move. When you first created your business plan, including a provision for fifty staff by the end of year three may have seemed a bit ambitious, and maybe it was. But what if your staff needs have increased to five hundred? Would the local market be able to satisfy your staff requirement, in terms of numbers and people available who have the skills that you require? Do keep an eye on other parts of the country, especially with regard to any grants that might be available for providing employment in certain areas.

Try another idea...

Trying to work out what will happen in three or more years is a difficult process, especially if you haven't even begun trading yet, but it does need to be done. To learn more, check out IDEA 5, *What's in your pocket?*

To prepare yourself for the possibility of massive growth over the coming three years it is time well spent to create 'dummy' financial projections to cover all of the possible scenarios. Using your existing financial projections as your template, alter the sales figures to reflect a growth of 100%, 500% and 1000% more than you are currently anticipating.

How did it go?

Q Isn't this just wishful thinking? Surely it would be better to concentrate on the realistic figures?

A *Yes and no. Assuming that your financial spreadsheets are easy to alter, the exercise itself will take no time at all. If the figures show that you require an additional member of staff for every 10% growth in turnover, for instance, you have gained some useful information.*

How did it go?

Q Is it worth showing these documents to a bank manager to help us borrow more money?

A *Probably not. Your original projections based on your market knowledge, the actual capital you have to spend, and the actual staff members you are currently employing will be the document upon which a lender will evaluate your business. These 'fantasy' projections are just tools to better understand your business.*

Q You say it won't take long, but I have spent days on these fantasy projections. It all seems to boil down to a massive increase in sales, but if sales were that great we would get competitors. How do I factor that in?

A *Imagine that you are a Martian, and distance yourself from these projections. You're right – a sudden burst in sales might not be sustainable because of competition and other factors. By careful analysis, you can work out various tactics to adopt at different stages in the process. For example, suddenly employing 500 people is a huge commitment, and requires additional finance. How would you obtain it? If sales crashed after six months, what would you do with all your people? Put your analysis in writing so that you can refer to it later as circumstances change.*

34

I'm all right Jack

Too many late nights, early mornings and not watching your diet can work when you're a student, but we're older now and we need to take care of ourselves.

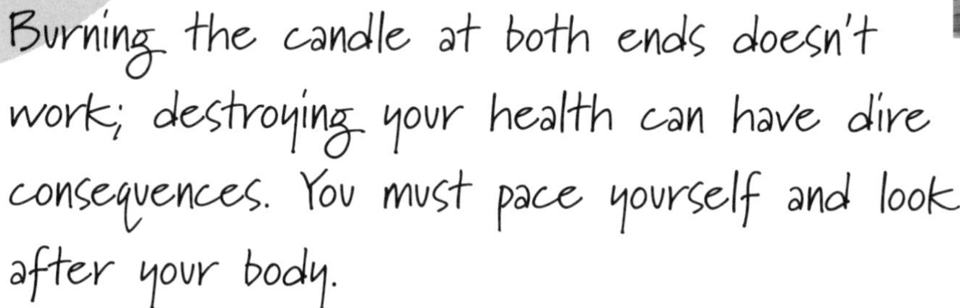

Burning the candle at both ends doesn't work; destroying your health can have dire consequences. You must pace yourself and look after your body.

In the heat of battle it is quite easy to forget about the basics in terms of your health and well-being – but launching a business can be and often is an incredibly stressful experience. The weight of responsibility and the meeting of self-declared targets affect the human body and mind in ways hitherto never experienced. Stress and burnout are certainly the buzzwords of the day in terms of the number of people taking extended leave away from their jobs, and whether half of them are really suffering with anything more than laziness is something that we can only guess at. However, that is not to belittle the fact that in some way, be it small or profound, the launching of your business will take its toll. Being aware of this is half the battle in stopping it from affecting you too much just when you need to be in tip-top condition and fully aware of your situation and surroundings.

Here's an idea for you...

Choose to spend one half-day a week with your family or friends away from your place of business. Choose a weekday and ensure that no meetings are ever scheduled during that time. Don't talk about the business, or your plans, or what happened in the morning. Just enjoy being with your people.

When planning a business you will be setting targets in terms of how much you need to make each month, how much you can spend and how many customers you hope to have served within a given amount of time. It is also important to set yourself targets for what you can achieve in any given day. Back-to-back meetings are sometimes an unavoidable necessity, but a week of them will take a toll on you and your performance. Try to balance your working week, even during the preparation of a business plan, so that you spread the load and fill your day with a variety of tasks requiring different skills, rather than working on a spreadsheet for eighteen hours in one single stint.

You hear it all the time: businesspeople complaining that there just isn't enough time in the day to eat properly. This might make them feel like martyrs and earn respect from certain other colleagues, but what is it really achieving? You can't expect to run the company car without putting in fuel, so why is your body any

Defining idea...

'A handful of patience is worth more than a bushel of brains.'
DUTCH PROVERB

different? Breaking for lunch or dinner is time not spent on the business, but you will be far more refreshed and energised to do quality work for hours afterwards with a nice meal digesting away inside you.

Try another idea...

If you will be working with anyone else, then it is important to know and understand his or her suitability for the role as much as understanding your own. To learn more, check out IDEA 42, *Surrounded by winners.*

You cannot ignore your long-suffering family. Creating a business can and often does become an obsession, but relationships with partners, family members and children cannot be turned on and off when you feel like it. Don't be a stranger in your home and make sure you put the business on hold every now and again to communicate with your nearest and dearest. Often a short break and concentrating on something completely different can recharge the batteries and prepare you for tomorrow far better than revising the business plan for the seventeenth time.

Keeping in shape doesn't have to mean a macho gym and squash programme. Do what you enjoy, not what is in fashion. If salsa dancing or rowing is what you enjoy, do it! Exercise should be fun if you are going to make it a regular habit.

Defining idea...

'Our patience will achieve more than our force.'
EDMUND BURKE

How did it go?

Q It really isn't viable for me to take an afternoon off during the week. If this business is not ready in time, the whole thing is in vain. Won't sometime at the weekend do?

A *No. This should be in addition to taking the Saturday or Sunday off – in retail or catering, this might be a Tuesday. The work will get done if you focus, and time off will help you to focus.*

Q My partner works full-time and my children are at school, so what's the point?

A *Time away is the point. If there really is no way of meeting up with family and friends, relax with a book or a film – or better yet, since you got all excited about your new business, when did you last clean the house?*

Q My partner has a stressful job and can't relax, so we're never relaxed when we're together. Frankly, I'd rather be at work!

A *Hmm...perhaps you both need to take a long, hard look at how to rearrange your lives. If your partner is earning a fortune and says that the stress is worth the money for another couple of years, maybe you should wait before launching the business. Or if you both think that the business is more important, perhaps your partner should get an easier job.*

35

Top of the pile

There are numerous competitions for businesses. If you win one or are even just short-listed, it could give your business additional exposure and put you on the map.

Business is about competing and to miss out on the opportunity of going toe-to-toe with other organisations in your industry is folly – or is it cowardice?

When setting up a business, entering a competition is probably the last thing on your mind, but it shouldn't be. You will probably have to be actually trading to be eligible, but why wait until then to complete the paperwork? Once you start trading you won't have time fill in application forms. Find out now what is on offer and get as prepared as you can – even if there are eleven months left before the deadline. You may well have to revise your figures slightly once the real customers start spending real money, but that is no more than an hour's work.

Here's an idea for you...

Scan the local papers and the internet for business competitions being run in your area. Usually they are city or countywide, although there are of course larger national and international awards up for grabs. If the deadline for entry is really too soon, or there is a requirement of having been trading for *x* months or years, be sure to note the next deadline for which you are applicable in your diary – otherwise you will forget.

WHAT DO THEY WANT?

In relative terms, very little. Often the application process requires you merely to provide documents that you will have already begun or completed: an executive summary, a business plan and some financial data. The judges are often looking for a professional vision and want to be convinced that your passion for the business can be realised. In some competitions the emphasis is on innovation or the use of web technology to change people's lives, but they are all looking for the same thing: a well-organised ship, clear direction and a hunger to win and be successful.

BUT WHY?

The application process will get your name known by the organisation administering the competition. Should your application be successful and your business is short-listed, you will begin to enjoy free promotional activity, which is never a bad thing. 'Best New Business of the Year' or whatever title the competition is operating under is a huge vote of confidence that you will be able to quote at every opportunity. Suppliers will take note, as will customers. If the competition is annual, then you have a whole year to ensure that everyone knows it was your business that beat all the others to the ground with a resounding slap. In certain cases (usually in nationwide or industry-specific competitions) there is prize-money or a development grant up for grabs – and as you know, any extra cash that finds its way into the coffers is always appreciated. For the prestige alone it is worth the time and effort to create a winning application. There is seldom a financial cost associated with entering, as the administration and prize-money (if applicable) is covered by grants or sponsorship. If you really think your business idea is that good, maybe others will too. Take an afternoon away from whatever you have planned and concentrate on entering your business into a competition.

Try another idea...

Entering business competitions is all about putting your business in direct competition with others. To learn more about the enemy, check out IDEA 27, *You're nothing!*

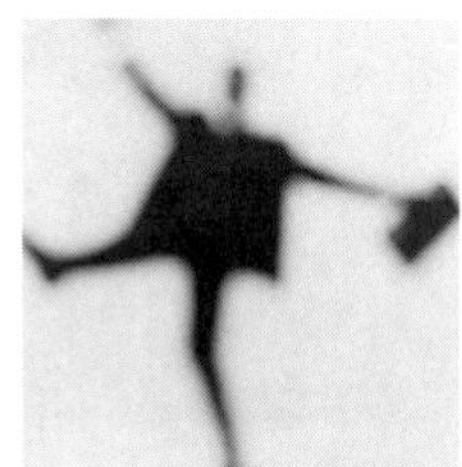

Defining idea...

'I've done the calculation and your chances of winning the lottery are identical whether you play or not.'

FRAN LEBOWITZ, author and poet

How did it go?

Q It still seems a lot of work. What if we don't get short-listed?

A *At worst, even if you are not successful you will have created a streamlined business plan and marketing material which can always be used in future competitions or edited to become copy for brochures.*

Q I can't see how we can apply without having traded for at least three years. What can I do?

A *Check the rules of entry. For new business awards especially, you won't be able to apply if you have been trading for more than two years! Hence the word 'new' in the title.*

Q I don't agree that these competitions are always great publicity. Don't you think that they sometimes look amateurish?

A *Pick the competitions that you think will suit your image. There's no point in entering 'best female entrepreneur under 25' if you are a 50-year-old man! Dig a little deeper, and look for competitions that have a good publicity machine and are professionally run.*

36

Buy it!

No matter how good your idea is, you must convince others to part with their cash to make it a success. Advertising your business will create awareness and 'help' customers buy from you.

Look for the cheapest ways to reach as many of your target audience as possible. Dragging people in off the street could work, but you might get in a bit of trouble with the police!

Newspaper advertising can be very effective but it can be very expensive over a prolonged period. The important thing for you to do is measure the effectiveness, if you can. Adding a reference code to specific adverts can help you monitor the effectiveness, as can counting the number of customers entering your premises before, during and after a campaign. No monitoring will ever give you an exact measure, but it should soon become apparent that advertising with a certain newspaper is working well or else is tantamount to burning twenty-pound notes.

Here's an idea for you...

If you are targeting the local press, be sure to focus on why the business is important for local people: are you going to be hiring locals, will it mean a boost to the economy, is it an exciting new venture for the local community to be proud of? Don't hold back, make the press release sing the praises of your town or city and guarantee yourself some free publicity.

Cinema advertising is a relatively cheap way to get great exposure for your business, no matter what your sphere of operations. For a fixed quarterly fee, a slide advertising your business is shown to cinema audiences before each feature film on a given screen. You can design the slide. Whether the film is an art house flick or a summer blockbuster, you reach a lot of people throughout the day and night. By nature of the seating in cinemas, audiences can't help but watch the slides change as they wait for the film. Whether you are running a restaurant, retail store or a firm of accountants, cinema goers transcend socio-demographic boundaries and you will be talking to your potential customers. Cinema advertising also has a perceived high value associated with it and therefore by nature of taking part you can win some kudos for your business. People do remember cinema ads.

Planning a series of adverts is generally more effective in terms of penetration and awareness, and you will get a better offer than the rate card on each advert by buying in bulk. By showing long-term loyalty to a paper or website (which may only be a four-week commitment) you begin to build a relationship and are much more likely to get a feature written about you in the future. While newspapers are supposed to be unbiased, the local papers are totally funded by advertising, and therefore advertisers can sway the mood of the editors because, quite simply, you are paying their wages.

Once you have launched a retail business, it is well worth creating flyers and employing students or friends to flyer around town during your first weeks of business. Many of the flyers will find there way into a nearby bin, but by ensuring that there is a simple map on the reverse, and an incentive such as '10% on presentation of this flyer', you can draw literally hundreds of customers to your business for minimal outlay.

Try another idea...

Awareness for your business does not always have to be paid for. To learn more check out IDEA 12, *Look at me!*

Do budget your advertising carefully and measure everything you can. Don't let costs spiral out of control, and make sure that you find out as quickly as possible what works and what doesn't. Don't forget the potential of free publicity; write a press release announcing your new business, no matter what stage you are up to. It is never too early to start letting the world know that you are on your way.

Defining idea...

'Advertising may be described as the science of arresting the human intelligence long enough to get money from it.'
ANONYMOUS

How did it go?

Q The paper is looking for some kind of commitment from us in terms of advertising before it will print the press release. At this stage I am unable to commit to a campaign. What can I do?

A *If you are going to be looking for staff, then don't commit to placing a promotional advert. Instead, promise to advertise your vacancies in the paper – rates for job adverts are much cheaper than generic advertising and it was something you would have done anyway.*

Q **We will be stocking high-value electronic products and the marketing manager would rather not announce to the locals that we are in town. The threat of burglary would be very high. Is she right to stop us advertising?**

A *The local undesirable fraternity are going to become aware of the contents of your warehouse whether you advertise the fact or not. Advertise anyway to get the knock-on benefits, and ensure that your building is protected.*

Q **A local design agency is quoting a fortune to prepare our materials, but one of our directors insists that we should use them. Should we spend the money?**

A *Graphic design is often grossly overpriced. Shop around, but make sure that the people you choose can deliver on time and to a high standard. Consider going abroad – there is no reason not to use overseas designers now that we have the internet. For example, I recently had to have a business card with my name and company details in Korean and English. The cost for the translation here was astronomical, so I had it done cheaply in the Far East. Watch out, though – you need a real Korean scholar to make sure that the transliteration of your name is suitably auspicious!*

PURCHASE THIS ITEM

340
350
S

37

Getting lost en route

You could do nearly no planning and still come out smelling of roses – but you'd be better off taking your chances on the Grand National. Make a plan!

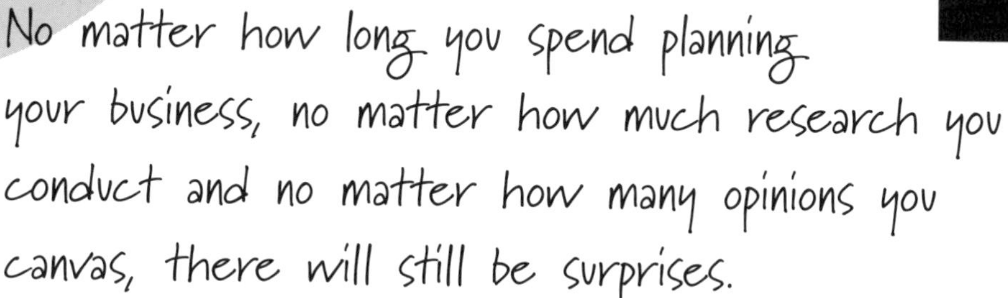

It's vital to diversify your offering and closely monitor the performance of your business. Not only will this avoid any nasty cash flow issues, but it will also help ensure that you are profiting from all of your sales channels.

There are occasions when the problem is much bigger than having to tighten your belt for a few months, or worse, laying off a member of staff to save costs. Unbelievably, it could be that your idea for a business just simply isn't working. It might be through no fault of your own, but the expenditure continues to grow and the income just hasn't quite got off the starting grid. This is when you need to have Option X.

Here's an idea for you...

It is worth an afternoon's time to consider how you would react should the worst case scenario actually happen. Plan for a change of direction after 3, 6 and 12 months. What equipment would you have already procured, how many staff would you be employing and what could you possibly do with your business should your master plan prove to be not that masterful?

Defining idea...

'If the facts don't fit the theory, change the facts.'
ALBERT EINSTEIN

OPTION X

Assuming that you have not yet lost the will to live, it's time to sit back and take stock of what it is you have achieved so far. Consider the potential your business would still have if you were to alter the offering slightly. By the time you consider an Option X, you will have no doubt invested heavily in facilities, business machinery, staff, training and stock of some description. Where else is there to go? Option X could be to change your offering from a retail outlet into a mail order/internet business. It could be to alter your customers from the public to trade customers or vice versa. You will know better what options are available to you, and the important thing is not to blinker your vision or let personal preference bias your decision.

LEAD BY EXAMPLE

A short case study: a TV programme once featured a shoe manufacturer in the north of England. For years they made sensible shoes and traditional work boots. Cobbling meant cash. Towards the end of the 1990s the business was facing fierce competition from other UK firms and cheap foreign imports. The firm employed a lot of people and did not want any of them to lose their jobs. What did they do? They looked at the skills within the firm and realised that there was still a need for handcrafted leather footwear. Work boots gave way to kinky boots and suddenly the firm was cash-rich once again producing high-quality thigh-length leather and PVC boots for blokes. This is not a joke! In a bid to save money, the managing director modelled the boots for men himself. They produced a high-quality catalogue, and started selling their enormous leather offerings at erotic trade-shows and to specialist retailers. The net result was that the company was turning over more than it had ever done, every job was saved, and more happy male customers were able to appreciate the joys of leather than ever before!

Try another idea...

A change of direction is extreme. To give yourself the best chance of success you will need to monitor what is happening day-to-day and week-to-week. To learn more, check out IDEA 49, *Time for reflection.*

Defining idea...

'What we call "Progress" is the exchange of one nuisance for another nuisance.'
HAVELOCK ELLIS, psychologist

How did it go?

Q Surely this doom and gloom philosophy is counter-productive to feeling confident about the actual business plan?

A *Not at all. It's always best to plan, and maybe Option X could prove to be another sales channel for your business or strong enough to become a separate company right from the outset.*

Q I am opening a hair salon. There aren't really that many options open to us should the business not work. Could it be that for some businesses there is no Option X?

A *There's always an Option X, just look harder. Could your stylists become mobile and service clients at home or in the office?*

Q I really think you are just being negative. Positive thinking always works, doesn't it?

A *No. Take the time to read about some business scandals and talk to some experienced businesspeople. Business is tough, and things can go wrong. By all means put on a cheerful face, but don't think that a winning smile is going to solve all your problems, any more than it would if you were caught in a snowstorm on Mount Everest. Be prepared, and make sure that you will survive!*

38

By any means necessary

The more routes to market you are able to tap into, the more chance you have of gaining revenue. Know what you want and go for it!

Talking about your great ideas for world domination down the pub is all very well, but your time would be better spent actually putting them into action.

Listing every possible sales channel may make for a healthy looking business plan, but don't spread yourself too thin. Each route to market will require expenditure, expertise and serious commitment. Know exactly why you are entering each route to market and what you expect to achieve from each sales channel. Many retailers never consider the possibility of mail order. Mail order, if you are already holding stock, is a relatively cheap way to expand your customer base. Start off small and local and test the market. If it works, grow to regional or national exposure at your own pace.

Here's an idea for you...

Seriously consider creating a part to your business that will explore either a reseller/lead generator scheme or a network-marketing scheme. There will be a cost associated with researching the market and carrying out the viability study, but sharing in what is already a multi-billion pound sales channel in the UK (and growing) has got to be worth it.

Defining idea...

'What we have to do is to be forever curiously testing new opinions and courting new impressions.'

WALTER PATER, 19th century writer

WEB FEST

The World Wide Web is an ever-growing phenomenon, and even despite the massive bursting of bubbles in 1999/2000 that many thought marked the end of a relatively short time in the limelight, selling through the internet can be a profitable endeavour. Research the web intensely, invest well in a website and reach a global audience at the switch of a button.

RESELLERS

You can also pay resellers or lead generators to help you sell products or services to customers, for a commission. Whether your resellers are web-based, 'real' people knocking on doors, or based in an office and drumming up trade by phone, it makes no difference – they are exposing your product or services to customers you were unlikely to come into contact with. Customers get what they want, the reseller earns a commission and you make money.

BUILDING A PYRAMID

Network marketing has become the new black in terms of alternative retail. From the early days of Avon ladies to Tupperware, we have moved on in leaps and bounds to the halcyon days of the noughties where we can now buy everything from perfume and bedtime accessories to cleaning products in the comfort of our own home, with very little effort. Effectively the shop is our living room and the sales assistant is a lifelong friend earning a bit of pin money on a Thursday night (or for the very successful, new cars and holidays).

Try another idea...

To understand alternative ways of bringing your product or service to market, check out IDEA 28, *Having peripheral vision.*

Setting up a network marketing scheme is well worth consideration, as long as your margins allow for the various commission structures and a multi-tiered hierarchy. Some products lend themselves very well to this, such as small items like perfume with a high margin, and others don't, such as large high-value items like rocking horses. Have your solicitor create the vendor contract and your accountant work with you on commissions and the organisational structure. Decide on the product and pricing and send your army off into the night to sell.

Defining idea...

'If you don't know where you are going, any road will take you there.'
LEWIS CARROLL

How did it go?

Q Our business will be based on selling financial products, not retailing. How can network marketing ever be an option?

A *Although the success stories so far have been companies selling retail products, there is nothing to say that a team of reps selling pensions will not work as effectively. Think outside of the box.*

Q We are planning to sell products that are already sold via network marketing. I would rather not compete. Isn't it better to stick with a chain of shops?

A *So there is someone else doing it. This probably means that they have researched it and feel the sales channel is viable. A bit of competition never hurt anyone. Consumers will love it, you indirectly benefit from the competitors' marketing and if you get your offering right, you could dominate the market in no time at all.*

39

VAT-baby

Most countries have some form of sales tax. Currently in the UK you do not have to become VAT registered until you or your business is turning over in excess of £58,000 p.a.

You can choose to become VAT registered if you wish, even if your turnover is much lower. It could save you a lot of money and even help your cash flow temporarily.

Paying VAT is simply unavoidable no matter what your drinking buddy says; they can and will catch you. Pleading ignorance is no excuse. Some individuals and businesses choose to become VAT registered long before they are turning over anywhere near the threshold precisely for the reason that it does give the impression that you are turning over at least £58,000 (in the UK). Being VAT registered means that you must quote your VAT registration number on all correspondence, which again for some people appears to give the individual or business more kudos or potential clout. By adding on VAT to an invoice it can give the impression of a more professional and longer-established business and, dare I say it, can mean that you are able to charge more for your work in the first place.

Here's an idea for you...

Call your local Customs & Excise office to understand your VAT obligations better. Surprisingly, the staff are friendly and will answer most questions immediately or get back to you with an answer if it is slightly more complex.

There is no such thing as no VAT. There are products (such as children's clothes, books and tampons) that are charged at 0% VAT, which does mean we as consumers don't pay anything, but the door is always open for that to change.

If you have not contacted an accountant, I would strongly recommend that you get in touch, if only to hear an explanation of VAT and how it will impact your business. I read about five guidebooks at the time of launching my first business and I think that I was more confused afterwards than I had been before. We were looking to retail toys and books; some were imported from EC countries, some from the Far East and some were manufactured in the UK. The combination of VAT applied at 17.5% and 0% was mind-boggling and I was pleased to pay someone else to deal with the headache.

As well as knowing and recording when and how much VAT to charge your customers, you must also keep account of the VAT your business has paid to others. If you become VAT registered you will have to submit a VAT return every quarter. Although you will be trusted with completing the empty boxes on the form, every now and again the figures will be queried by Customs & Excise and you will be asked to show proof. Ordinarily you will be asked to show specific

Defining idea...

'Income tax returns are the most imaginative fiction being written today.'
HERMAN WOUK, author

invoices and receipts to ensure that the figures tally. Accountancy software such as Sage will assist you with this menial but important task. At the end of the day Customs & Excise would much rather you asked 'obvious' questions before submitting your VAT return. Bear in mind that if your returns are consistently incorrect, this can actually lead to a stretch in your local prison. The good news is that, now and again, especially when you are first starting up a business, your VAT liability is actually a negative and you get a cheque from them – but this is never sustainable because it means you are spending more money than you are receiving.

Try another idea...

Be sure to account for your VAT liability whether you are VAT registered or not for the real cost of setting up your business. Many organisations selling to the trade or providing services quote their prices exclusive of VAT – adding on a whopping 17.5% to your expenditure will make a huge difference to your projections. **To learn more, check out IDEA 6, *Cheap at twice the price.***

Defining idea...

'The avoidance of taxes is the only intellectual pursuit that carries any reward.'
JOHN MAYNARD KEYNES

How did it go?

Q I am not really sure what questions I should ask the VAT man. Where's a good place to start?

A *You will never receive the answer if you don't know the question. Take the plunge and contact an accountant to get you going. They will probe you about your business and you will soon have five or six queries that will need to be answered by Customs & Excise before you will be able to trade.*

Q How do I know whether the benefits associated with opting to become VAT registered outweigh the negatives?

A *There are no real negatives. Filing a VAT return, assuming your accounts are in order, is literally just hitting a button on the computer. If you are planning for your business to be truly successful and set you up for life, you are probably going to need to turnover more than £58,000 per year and therefore it is better to get the practice in early and become registered from day one. One exception is if you are self-employed, don't claim many expenses and don't expect to earn £58,000 per year, in which case the cost and time of being VAT registered might outweigh the savings – but ask your accountant for advice.*

40

The selling game

For you to sell, you will need someone else to buy. You need special tactics to get them in through the door and ensure you have the most payment options.

A till full of coins simply isn't good enough anymore; there is a lot more to working in retail than a cashbox and a smile.

An A-frame is such a simple little device, and there really isn't a more effective way to block pedestrians, cause major issues for the older population and amuse kids who can't help but kick the things over – but that said, they work. A-frames are a backup facility to catch the attention of customers who are actually looking where they are walking, rather than over their shoulder at what they are passing. Just covering an A-frame with your logo, an arrow and a tagline will catch people's attention and, if you happen to be a little bit off the beaten track, draw customers from busy pedestrian streets over to you. There are some local councils who get a bit upset about the use of A-frames but the simple rule of thumb is that if you see others using them, then the chances are that you'll be OK. Just make sure you don't put them on the road.

Here's an idea for you...

Don't feel obliged to sign up with your current bank for your credit card processing facility. Look around for the best deal. Remember that banks should be competing for your business, not the other way round – find the deal that best works for you.

GRAFFITI ON THE WALLS

Let everyone know you are opening for business just as soon as you have keys to your premises. There is a school of thought that strongly believes in covering up windows with a soapy whitewash until launch. I think that this gives the wrong impression and could mistakenly lead to potential customers thinking that your company has closed down or moved on, rather than being the new face in town.

Whatever space is available to you for signage, use it to the maximum. It's all very well being minimalist and softly spoken inside the shop, but outside you need to use every single tactic to gain the attention of hapless shoppers. Shout as loud as you can. Bear in mind the large numbers of customers who will be given vague directions such as 'the toy shop near Marks' or 'it's a lovely little place just down from The Bear'. Be your own beacon and light up the path to salvation.

TAKING PLASTIC

It is imperative in this day and age that you offer your customers the ability to pay by debit and credit cards. Very few people now carry around large amounts of cash and, although there is a cost associated with hiring the machinery and a per-transaction charge for every purchase, customers will not be too amused if they have to leave the queue, go to a cash point, and then come back to pay for their items – in fact, they won't do it!

Each bank will offer its own card machine and will accept a varying range of cards. When making a choice try to marry up the least expensive in terms of running costs and the option that gives your customers the most choice. As well as the Visa and MasterCard options there are a whole host of other card issuers out there: Solo, Electron, Delta, Switch to name but a few.

Try another idea...

More and more retailers are looking to the internet as the next trading frontier. To learn more about the web, check out Chapter 45, *Playing with the electric internet.*

SHOW AND TELL

Once you have entered into an arrangement with a bank and are now able to accept credit and debit cards, along with the machinery you will receive a few stickers and plaques showing the cards that you now accept. Be sure to stick them up near the door and till points – they are a little ugly but it saves having to verbally list the cards to every other shopper.

Defining idea...

'One essential to success is that your desire be an all-obsessing one, your thoughts and aims be co-ordinated, and your energy be concentrated and applied without letup.'
CLAUDE M. BRISTOL, author

How did it go?

Q The bank I approached offers the best per-transaction rates and monthly fee but would prefer if all of my banking were through them. To open a merchant account only, they want me to pay a large surcharge. What should I do?

A *Your projected income will quickly determine the answer. If your level of trading is likely to be very low, then pay the slightly higher per-transaction fee with your existing bank. It will be cheaper. If, however, you are projecting tens of thousands of pounds worth of business, then the surcharge is a drop in the ocean.*

Q The bank offering the best rates is happy to accept every card under the sun, some of which I have never heard of. Should we offer to accept all of these card types?

A *Yes! The more choice and convenience you can offer your customers, the more likely they are to buy from you and enjoy the experience. Don't just consider the card providers you carry in your own wallet – think global.*

WHO ARE YOU?
I'M YOUR WORST NIGHTMARE, PAL

41

Big brother

Your accounts are likely to be audited once a quarter or once a year. It is never a walk in the park, but you can make the experience at least bearable by being prepared.

No, that big pile of paperwork strewn in the corner does not constitute filing! Get box files and get organised.

An auditor is appointed to ensure that what you have reported in your quarterly or annual accounts is in fact a true and honest representation of the year's financial activity. They will either work in your office or take the documentation they require away with them and report back in a couple of weeks. Auditors aren't trying to catch you out, unless of course you really are doing something a little bit naughty like buying timeshares in France with company money. They are just making sure that the payments you made went to the right beneficiary and the receipts you took were for the correct amount and ended up in the correct account. The more helpful you are with their enquiries, the quicker the whole thing will be over with.

Defining idea...

'When two men in business always agree, one of them is unnecessary.'

WILLIAM WRIGLEY, JR, king of gum

Here's an idea for you...

Work through all of the invoices you have paid and ensure that they have all been logged in your accounting records, that you can find the corresponding debit from your bank account, and that all the invoices are those actually received from the company providing the service or product, not notes written on scrap-paper. You will save yourself a lot more time in the long run by correcting problems now.

GET THE SOFTWARE

There are very few companies that continue to manually record their accounts in double-entry ledger books. Although this works fine, it is not very time efficient and doesn't allow multiple users to be inputting financial data simultaneously. From a security point of view it is harder to 'cook' the electronic books because programs like Sage record every transaction, even if it is later edited or deleted. The benefits of using accountancy software are speed, quick access to data and the ability to import and export figures, graphs and reports at the push of a button. Your accountant will advise on their preferred software and they will be happy to receive disks, printouts and reports generated by your software to work on.

Like anything, if you keep on top of it, the workload required is minimal. However, if you let your accounts slip, even for a month, the molehill soon becomes a mountain and rushing to catch up is often when mistakes occur. As a rule of thumb, try to keep your software up to date with entries at least every third day. As soon as your bank statements arrive, reconcile them. By doing this you will be able to spot discrepancies very quickly.

Defining idea...

'There's no business like show business, but there are several businesses like accounting.'
DAVID LETTERMAN

ENSURING CLARITY

An audit is not dissimilar to due diligence and therefore if you have prepared for one, you have prepared for the other. To learn more check out IDEA 24, *Surviving due diligence*.

Try another idea...

You will have a good idea which questions the auditor is going to ask: they will be the questions you are hoping they don't ask. Sudden or strange purchases that seem very high value and likewise sudden spikes in sales that don't seem to fit the mean pattern will raise an eyebrow. Any payments made to either yourself or staff members not related to salary or wages will also catch the eye of an auditor, and if the payment was related to expenses it is imperative that you have the corresponding receipts. Don't throw anyway anything and give it a home in a box.

How did it go?

Q I simply haven't got time to go through all of this right now. Can't I hire a temp?

A *If you made the majority of the purchases then you are going to be able to do the job quicker and more accurately. Any third party you are intending to involve will be asking questions and taking up your time clarifying minor points.*

Q Why not wait until the actual audit and then simply retrieve the invoices/receipts or bank statements in question?

A *Because it is never that easy. The one piece of paper they ask for will be the one that had coffee spilt on it and was destroyed six months ago. Don't leave things to the last minute and risk making the assessors suspicious, or risk not providing the information in time for the submission of your annual accounts.*

42

Surrounded by winners

Never hire out of pity – feeling sorry for someone might make you sleep better for a few nights but having a great team will help you sleep well for years!

Your organisational structure should be a pyramid, not a flat line. If others want to lead so much, let them set up their own business.

They say a strong business is only as strong as the people working for the business – and it's true, whoever they are. There really is only so much that one person can do, and you will have to hire staff to help you realise your business ambitions. What we are all looking for when hiring staff is versions of ourselves who are quite easy to mould and as passionate about the business as we are. This seldom happens. Every person is unique and no one will be 'perfect' for the job. If you can see beyond this, there are a lot of highly talented individuals out there who will work very hard and assist you in making the business a success. Look for a drive to succeed. You need to surround yourself only with winners who *will* make it happen.

Here's an idea for you...

Work on the assumption that there will be a manager of some description for every five staff you employ. Make it clear in terms of salary and benefits that the rank of management does have its perks, and to make it easier in terms of planning costs, separate management staff from rank and file on the financial projections. As your staff numbers grow, you will notice a huge hike in costs, but if you hire well, the costs incurred paying good managers will be returned many times over in excellence.

Defining idea...

'The greatest of faults, I should say, is to be conscious of none.'
THOMAS CARLYLE

There is no hard and fast way to assure this, but during the interview process you should be hunting like-minded individuals who remind you a little bit of yourself.

Anyone you are considering employing as a manager should be not only competent at his or her own job, but should share part of your vision and passion for the business. A consideration should always be: if you and the other senior managers were out of the office, would you trust this person to represent the business as well as yourself? Or would you be embarrassed for them to be involved in any meeting and much rather they hid in a box for a few hours? If you have any doubts, don't give them the title of manager. With regard to organisational structure, you must also steer clear of silly titles and giving the person who makes coffee the title of operations manager or director of services. This serves no purpose other than confusion.

STRETCHING YOURSELF AND OTHERS

Every business will have different staffing needs, but assuming you are launching a small to medium-sized enterprise there will be a level of middle management that can act as your eyes and ears, and to an extent, your three-line whip in terms of getting the most out of your staff. There's a strange philosophy that holds sway in some places that long hours equate to hard work. It is simply not true. It is far better to have your staff working diligently for a seven-hour day than to have an army of sycophants hanging around the office from dawn until dusk (and later) doing nothing in particular. Be fair on yourself and your staff when setting working hours, but expect hard work in return. If you are paying a fair to good wage then it is your right to demand excellence.

To get the most out of your staff you need to know what it is you want. To learn more check out IDEA 25, *Know thyself*.

Try another idea...

'Success is relative. It is what we can make of the mess we have made of things.'
T.S. ELIOT

Defining idea...

How did it go?

Q The new financial projections show that my employment costs will increase by about 20% if there is a manager for every five members of staff. How is this sustainable?

A *If your managers are working well they will be motivating and encouraging your staff to perform every day; in theory your extra costs will be set off by increased productivity. Don't just hire staff in February because you planned to in the projections, hire them when the income of the business and the workload justifies it.*

Q In the financial services industry, the job title is everything. I will have to issue my staff with manager and director titles for them to be taken seriously by their clients and colleagues. How can I alter the trend?

A *If the titles must be given and everyone in the office is a manager of this or a director of that, be sure that they do have a responsibility to justify the title as well as their primary role. They could be quite mundane tasks, but someone needs to be in charge of the stationery cupboard and someone else needs to be in charge of the kitchen, etc. Otherwise all of these jobs will be left to you!*

43

Who are you?

It can sometimes prove very difficult to judge your own ability. Constantly appraise your abilities realistically and try to compare them with those of others in your field.

The size of your office compared to that of your former boss will not tell you much, although it's nice to know he would be green with envy if he saw your gilt-edged staplers!

A can-do attitude is absolutely paramount to build a business up from pitch to profitability. Confidence in yourself and your proposal will get the business off the ground and drive you to continue late into the night and long after everyone else has clocked off. Working for yourself is in itself a huge motivator and if you have come this far then the rest is academic. There will be setbacks and lows which take strength of character to overcome, but that's why you got involved in this project in the first place – to prove to yourself that you could do it. Announcing that you plan to launch a business often results in words of warning and concern from those nearest and dearest to you. If you read too much into statistics then there is far more chance that your business will fail than succeed. There is a risk associated with starting a business, but there is also a risk to crossing a busy road.

Here's an idea for you...

Invite a former colleague out for dinner. You will be surprised at how willing people are to help and get involved in your project. Within an hour you should be up to speed with everything that has happened since your departure, what's new, who's new and who's in the firing line. Information like this is priceless and will help you gain new clients and avoid potential mistakes.

Knowing when to ask for help will lead to your business succeeding. We all have our limitations, some more than others, but there is no shame or failure in holding your hands up and requesting assistance. Just as Rome wasn't built in a day, it was not built by one person. You will need the help of your colleagues, family and friends to start a business. To try and block all assistance is not only detrimental, it is downright rude and arrogant. We are constantly learning new things from others, and starting a business is no different. Defining yourself fit for the task is as much about knowing what you can't do alone as it is knowing what you are capable of.

Launching your own business, for a matter of months if not years, can be an all-consuming eat-as-much-as-you-like buffet of self-indulgence and isolation. In your previous career, working in another company, you will have kept aware of what else is going on in the industry and which companies are doing what. Concentrating on your own business is obviously a priority but don't lose contact with those you used to work with and keep up those subscriptions to the industry press. Don't push for information if it is not forthcoming but a tactical night out with former colleagues can

Defining idea...

'Nothing endures but personal qualities.'
WALT WHITMAN

reveal what new innovations your former company is planning, who the movers and shakers are, and possible leads for future clients and ideas for your own business. This may sound somewhat mercenary, and it is – this is business.

Try another idea...

In time it won't be just you making the business happen, so surround yourself with like-minded individuals and effective staff. To learn more, check out IDEA 42, *Surrounded by winners.*

How did it go?

Q The exercise feels a bit like spying. Is this Machiavellian attitude completely necessary?

A *Information gathering and dissemination wins most wars; you're not being amoral, just keeping a competitive advantage.*

Q My former boss was happy to help on the advice front, but is less willing to divulge company information now that I am no longer staff. Was the exercise wasted?

A *Not at all, keeping a network of contacts is always advisable, especially if you are launching a business within the same industry. At the end of the day, you received the advice you needed and I'm sure the few drinks you had went down a treat...*

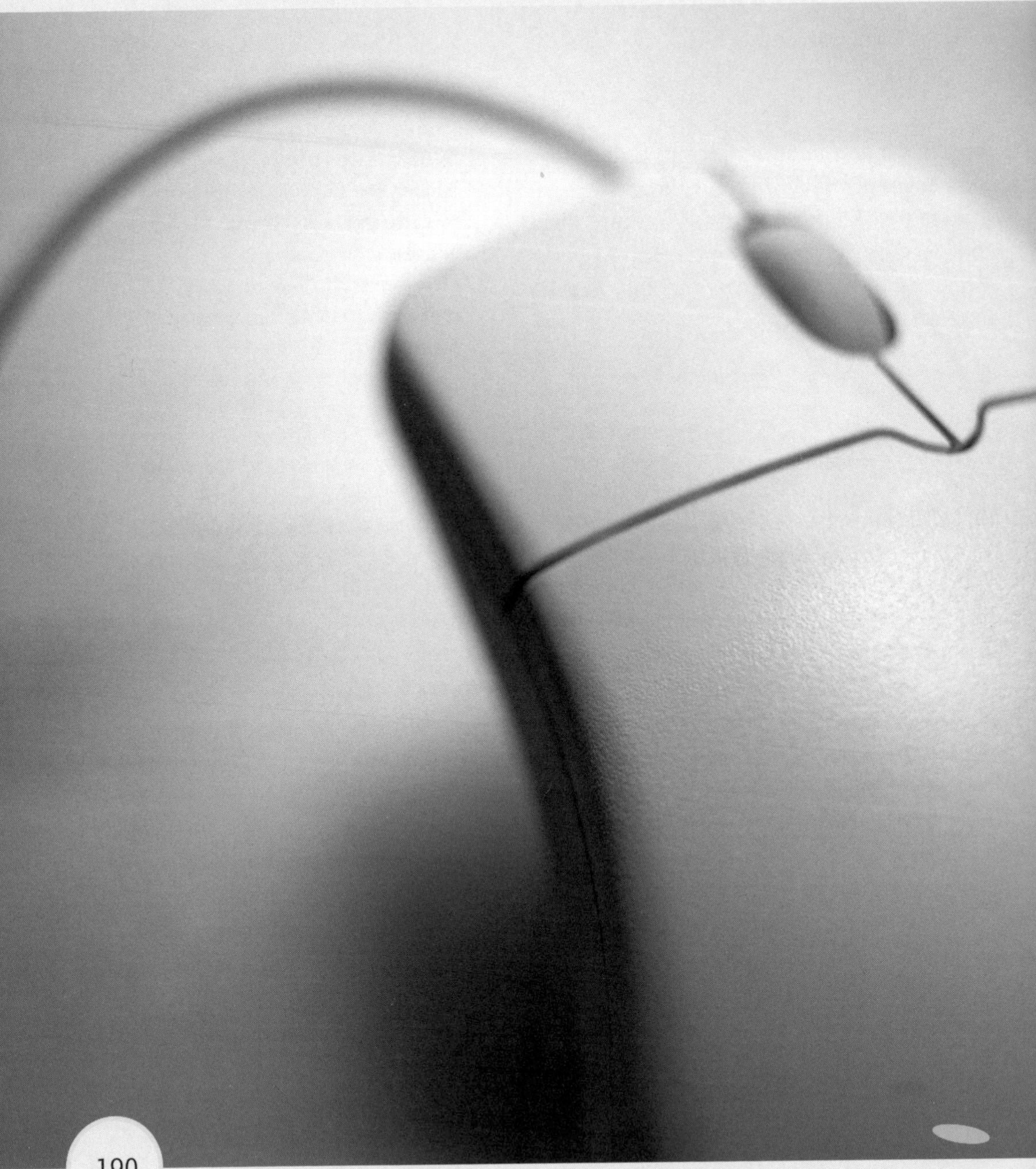

44

The soft machine

Like them or loath them, computers are everywhere and to submit documents not created with software makes you look behind the times.

All new computers now come with a software bundle of some description, but there are no free lunches and you'll need to go shopping for more.

Computers have become so mainstream that many of us have practically forgotten how to do proper joined-up writing with a pen. There are armies of the very young and very old surfing the web and submitting their 'What I did on my holidays' essay in word-processed type. Knowing what software to buy or download can be a minefield; the simple rule is to work with what you know but keep your eyes open for improvements.

Here's an idea for you...

List the ancillary software you have downloaded from the internet, such as Adobe Acrobat Reader (allowing you to read secure documents saved as Acrobat files). By ensuring that every PC (or Mac) has the same suite of software, your staff will be able to work on any machine and you will minimise problems should one machine crash.

THE BASICS

Every business is going to need a word-processing package to compile letters, invoices and most importantly your business plan. Microsoft certainly has a lot to answer for, but there's no denying that their operating systems and Office software is the most recognised. By installing Office you will be able to communicate with most other users and companies. Office will give you an email client (Outlook), spreadsheet software (Excel), word-processing capabilities (Word), a reasonably powerful database (Access), and the ability to create presentations (PowerPoint). If you need to create flowcharts or system maps, then Visio is your boy. For the in-depth planning of projects there's Microsoft Project, and when your business is almost running itself and you fancy an afternoon off dominating the ancient world, you'd do well to install 'Age of Mythology'. For accountancy software there is a whole host of options available and the size of your business (or your accountant) will probably dictate which software best fits. Sage, in my view, is a good all rounder.

HIDDEN TALENTS

There is now a piece of software to do pretty much anything, from designing labels for envelopes to designing and typesetting books, all for the home or small office user. As with the price of hardware, the price of software is now very affordable. Quite simply the more packages you and your staff are able to use, the more money you will save. When hiring, no matter what the role is, be sure to find out what software packages your future employee can use. A business that can work independently with data and images and can produce effective results and presentable information is very strong indeed.

Try another idea...

No business is truly embracing the digital age without its own website. To learn more, check out IDEA 45, *Playing with the electric internet.*

GOT A LICENCE FOR THAT?

The avoidance of paying for software licences can be a short-term gain financially but you and your business will be running a huge risk. It is often tempting to install the same piece of software onto multiple machines with only a single-user licence. In the vast majority of cases you might well get away with it. But the software manufacturers do come down hard on you if you are caught and are wising up to the fact by insisting that your software is registered online before it becomes fully operational. Buy the multiple-user licence and sleep better at night. Take a software audit off the main machine in the business. List each and every piece of software installed on your machine and ensure that you install the same software on to any further computers purchased.

Defining idea...

'The most overlooked advantage to owning a computer is that if they foul up there's no law against wacking them around a little.'
JOE MARTIN, cartoonist

How did it go?

Q One of my staff prefers to use a different email client to me. Is this a problem?

A *Only when things go wrong. It is best to have one email package across the business, so that when things go wrong they can be fixed easily. Only allow staff to use software that can be easily supported in-house.*

Q The developers need some software that the rest of us cannot use, why should we install it onto our machines?

A *Software should be installed on at least one other machine as a backup, in case the first machine goes down. Having extra software on your machine will not affect its performance, but having a member of staff who is unable to work will affect your business.*

45

Playing with the electric internet

Website promotion should encourage progress and growth of you or your company; a perfect promotional website will do both of these things.

Attract your users with a slick, well-executed website. Don't slap them in the face with a wet kipper.

Every Tom, Dick and Harry is trying to promote, sell, force their views, convert, inspire, turn on and sometimes steal from hapless users of the World Wide Web. To decide that you want no part in the madness is terribly honourable but not terribly bright. It really is a case of: *if you can't beat 'em, join 'em and then beat 'em*. Promoting yourself, your product or your views on the web can be expensive and ineffectual and it can also be so viral and successful that you will be overwhelmed with demand. But when you are up against all of this noise on the internet, how are you going to rise above and ensure that your site shouts loudest without puncturing eardrums?

Here's an idea for you...

Ask these questions about your website: Is there a message to be conveyed? Are you conveying it? Are you reinforcing it? If the answer is yes to all, you are on your way to creating the perfect promotional website.

Web users, by and large, are promiscuous – they will use your site for only as long as it continues to please them. When they've had their fill (or what they perceive to be all you have to offer) they move on to the next site. It is in those short few minutes, or seconds, depending on your performance (noticing any parallels here?), that you have the opportunity to hook them.

WHY PROMOTIONAL SITES WORK

The best promotional websites are those that don't confuse. They are clear in their message about what they are promoting, whether that be an organisation (e.g. financial services), a specific product (e.g. a new drink), or a concept (e.g. druid baptisms). The site, no matter how large, is geared towards this one purpose and no matter which page of the site your user visits, they understand.

Defining idea...

'When I took office, only high energy physicists had ever heard of what is called the World Wide Web...Now even my cat has its own page.'
BILL CLINTON

You can still show depth and breadth within a promotional site, but this should not all be crammed onto the homepage. Let your navigational options guide the visitor to where they want to go and let users travel at their own pace.

WHY PROMOTIONAL SITES DON'T WORK

The worst promotional websites are those that try to alert the user to absolutely everything on the homepage. The site's owner feels that they are showcasing their entire offering; the visitor gets frightened, somewhat confused and leaves. More commonly, a website will be full of claims reinforcing quality, excellence, excitement and professionalism – yet the actual site is slow, badly designed and maintained. From this, the user will be quick to judge – the only thing being promoted is your incompetence. Not the desired effect.

To complement your web offering you must ensure that your office is running all the right software. To learn more check out IDEA 44, *The soft machine*.

Try another idea...

Think of your favourite drink – alcoholic or otherwise. If you were designing a micro-site for that company, what messages would you want to convey? How would you promote that product and why? With the results, formulate a list of core messages – so 'not over fizzy' would become 'competitive advantage' and 'tastes great on ice or straight' would become 'expanding market'.

Q We are in an industry with very large players who can spend far more on their web design that we can. How can we possibly compete with their level of spend?

How did it go?

A *Good web design does not always mean high cost – work within your budget and make sure the message is clear. If people like what you are promoting, they will use your services and tell their friends. If you don't promote well you will lose out, and that has nothing to do with competitors having more money to spend.*

Q Our website is promoting a completely new concept. Is it not better to break with convention?

A *You can be as original or zany in your concepts as you like, but there are still conventions that should be adhered to if you want people to notice your site and feel inclined to read on. Let the text or the images explain the concept, but the rules of promotion do not alter – explain to the user what it is, let them contact you for more information and don't confuse.*

Q We would love to advertise our products in our own way. Unfortunately the manufacturers dictate how their items are featured on our website. Will this hinder us?

A *It can be a blessing when a manufacturer dictates image sizes, colours and other specifications. Work with them on it. If they demand you only use their information (product details and images/logo, etc.) then make sure they provide the graphics/text as they like it. They will also be able to help you in the promotion of your site, by advertising you on their site/literature as an approved retailer. So, although they might hinder or impede your overall design, they will have advice, resources and access to potential customers you wouldn't normally come across – all for using a specific pantone or tagline within your website.*

46

Staplers and shredders

Save company money by hiring well and running a tight ship, not making five people share a half-chewed ballpoint pen.

No matter what your business, there are some basics that you simply cannot be without. Yes, it's time to go shopping again.

You know the importance of gaining information about the industry, new developments and your competitors. On the flip side of this, you have also got to protect information about your business, your staff and your customers. Insisting on a high level of care, with regard to the storage of documents, is not being a control freak – it's common sense and, in certain cases, a legal requirement. Organisation starts with the safe filing of physical documents in a suitable location, i.e. in box-files under lock and key. With regard to electronic data, this should be backed up as often as possible and sensitive information should always be password protected. A shredder may at first seem to be a luxury, but it is an essential for each and every business.

Here's an idea for you...

Take the time to set up an account with one of the many national office suppliers. Competition is fierce, which is good for you, the consumer; prices are much lower than in the high street and you don't have to spend very much at all to enjoy free same-day delivery. By setting up your account immediately you will be able to save from day one and have 30 days to pay.

No matter how innocuous a random printout or scrap of paper may seem, it can reveal an awful lot. Shred everything (except, of course, your accounts right before an audit!).

A WELL-STOCKED CUPBOARD

A business must provide the facilities your staff need to operate effectively. Simple items of stationery do add up and for a paperless office you will be staggered by how much paper a small business can get through. Skimping on the basics is not cost effective if a member of staff is wasting time hunting for the one office stapler or the company post-it note. Continue to ask your staff what they require to help them work more efficiently. Be sure that you or another member of staff is monitoring the stationery cupboard, both in terms of who is using what and how much is left.

INK AND LASERS

Another false economy we've all been guilty of is the inkjet printer. Often a printer manufacturer will get into bed with a computer manufacturer and provide an inkjet printer for next to nothing with every new PC/Mac. Not to seem wasteful, we plug the printer in and away we go. After what seems like two sheets of printed paper, they're out of ink, and so it begins. There is a good reason that inkjet printers are given away for next to nothing – ink refills cost an absolute fortune. It may pain you to see the prices of laser printers, but the long-term savings you'll make are astronomical. Take the plunge, buy a laser printer and enjoy a faster machine that costs far less to run.

Try another idea...

As well as the bits and pieces you will need for your business to operate effectively, there will also be a need for larger-value items that form the infrastructure of your business. **To learn more, check out IDEA 10, *System addict*.**

Defining idea...

'All programmers are playwrights and all computers are lousy actors.'
ANONYMOUS

How did it go?

Q I applied to open an account and the representative said they would have to run a credit check. If I haven't been trading, will the business fail the check?

A *Unlikely. The credit check is a standard procedure to ensure you haven't been running up huge bills with other organisations. If you have yet to start trading your record should be clean.*

Q The office supplier I chose offers both a catalogue/phone ordering facility and a Web ordering facility. Which is best?

A *Their website will have all of the latest prices and offers and sometimes even a web discount. It is cheaper for the office supplier to receive orders via the web and often those savings are passed on to you.*

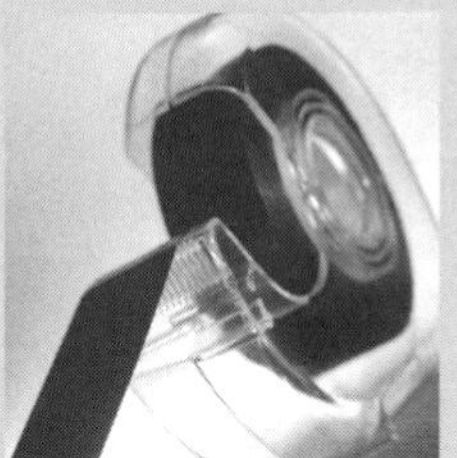

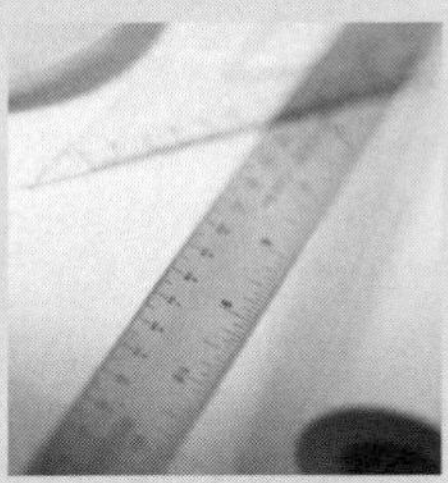

47

World domination

Assessing risk is laborious, but the entrepreneur must be prepared for every eventuality, no matter how obscure and unlikely it might seem.

It is highly unlikely that your building will burn down, but that's not to say these things don't happen. You're not tempting fate, merely remembering to bring an umbrella.

BUSINESS MACHINERY

If your business relies on computers and software to any degree, and there are very few businesses nowadays that do not, then you must acknowledge that they are temperamental, likely to crash, or corrupt, or fall over at the most inopportune moment possible. What does that actually mean for you and your business? To lose a document because you have failed to save it is incredibly annoying and will have you in an inconsolable rage for hours – to lose the data contained on an entire machine, or worse, a server, is not only heartbreaking, but also actually damaging to the business. Back up everything and ensure the backup disks or tapes are securely stored.

Here's an idea for you...

If you haven't already, create a section in your business plan outlining the risks associated with your business. The risk list should incorporate everything from what happens if you lose key members of staff to your reliance upon third party capital in terms of setting up and running the business. In a way you are listing your business weaknesses, but hiding your head in the sand will not convince anyone you actually know what you are doing.

THE ACTIONS OF OTHERS

For businesses that rely upon a network or internet connection to operate effectively, be prepared for a loss of connection. With the millions of miles of cables and pipes that criss-cross the country a couple of feet below the surface of the road, it is not uncommon for a JCB or industrious worker armed with a pneumatic drill to sever your connection to the World Wide Web. Ensure that there is an SLA (service level agreement) with your provider and you have plans in place to rectify the problem should a loss of connection occur.

PROTECTING YOUR BUSINESS

Staff contracts are there to protect both employee and employer. Although we have all moved on to new pastures in our time, as will your staff, you have the right and responsibility to ensure that your staff must serve a notice period (so that you can find a replacement with minimal disruption) and that they do not take sensitive information with them. The level of the role will often determine a suitable notice period and monitoring email communications will deter a member of staff from 'sharing' confidential documents with other companies or individuals.

WHICH 'WHAT IF'?

There are obviously too many 'what ifs' to list them all. When compiling a list it is important to be realistic in your assessment. You don't have to get bogged down in detail and specify that you fear an attack from six youths, wearing red, on a Thursday night, but you can acknowledge the threat of terrorism or sabotage to the premises. Again, you are not required to list each member of staff and the impact should one or all leave, but you should acknowledge that losing key members of staff would have an impact on the business.

Acknowledging the risk and noting it down, especially within the business plan, is incredibly wise, but you must also be prepared for what you might need to do to rectify the situation. **To learn more, check out IDEA 51, *The Poseidon adventure.***

Try another idea...

'All generalizations are dangerous, even this one.'
ALEXANDRE DUMAS

Defining idea...

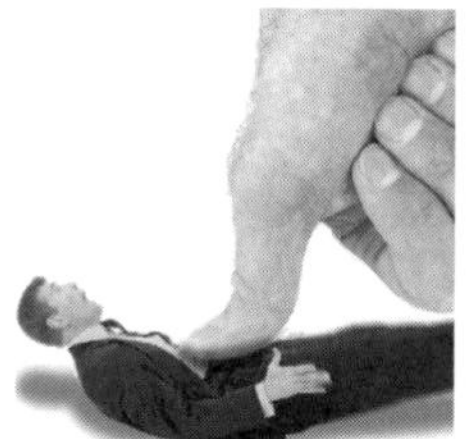

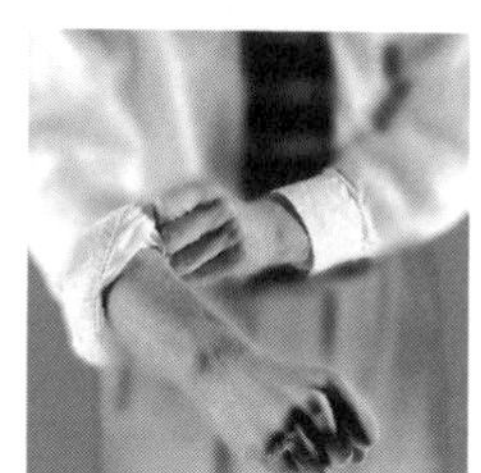

How did it go?

Q There are a number of risks we have listed which, in terms of our business, would be catastrophic. We have no solution to some of the problems. What should we do?

A *There are some risks that would be incredibly damaging, if the scenario occurred, and you will struggle to find a solution. Worry not, this exercise is all about acknowledging the risk to show that you have considered the problem; there probably isn't a simple solution.*

Q I feel that I am important to the business. Would it be arrogant to suggest that me leaving the business is a risk?

A *Not at all, especially if your business is a limited or public limited company. The board and shareholders will read this document and it is important that they recognise your importance to the continued success of the operation.*

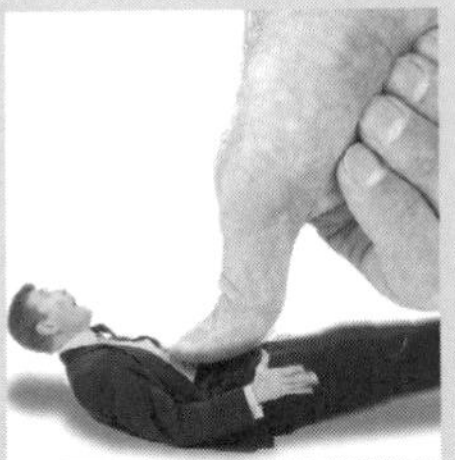

48

What are you crying about?

Customers can be annoying, needy and very time consuming, but without them you would not have a business. Are you nurturing your customers?

The best people to judge how well your business is performing are those whom you are selling to. Take a deep breath and start proactively interacting with your customers.

Always keep questionnaires and correspondence to customers polite and well written, and answer their questions fully – you don't want your rude letters to be shown for all to see on some tough-talking consumer affairs programme on TV!

Many businesses deal with dissatisfied customers reactively – nothing happens until the complaint comes that orders have not been received, the product was faulty or the wrong item was received. Customers get upset if they perceive the staff to be rude or the service they receive to be less than satisfactory. The situation is usually dealt with and everyone concerned is happy for a very short period of time.

Here's an idea for you...

Any time you have contact with a customer, it is an opportunity to sell to them. Try to think of ways that you can use the customer complaints process in your marketing. For example, if you solve someone's complaint to their satisfaction, it is a great moment to ask them if they want to see a new catalogue, obtain a quantity discount on their next purchase, or come to a product launch.

Defining idea...

'Your most unhappy customers are your greatest source of learning.'
BILL GATES

All of this additional customer contact time, whether it is additional phone calls, emails or full-blown rows in the shop or office, is valuable time when you or your staff are not getting on with the job.

It is much better to pre-empt your customers and ask them for ways that you could improve your business. Make their experience in dealing with you more problem-free and even fun.

A QUESTION FOR YOU

When it comes to airing views, customers are often happy to give positive feedback as much as negative comments. The trick is devising a system that will coax the information out of them. But before you can start sending questionnaires to your customers, you need to know what it is you are asking. When approaching customers for feedback, be as specific as possible. Asking customers or clients whether they like your business will result in very bizarre answers, and although you will be happy that Mrs Dwyer thinks the young girl on reception is wonderful because she has the same colour eyes as her daughter, you have only succeeded in wasting everybody's time. Be clear what it is you are assessing. How satisfied are you with the service you receive from us? How satisfied are you with our pricing? Allow users to mark you out of 5 and also allow for extra comments at the end of the questionnaire. Try not to ask more than seven questions if you are not compensating clients for their time.

Sometimes a questionnaire can reveal fundamental problems. It can be very demoralising but very insightful. The important thing is how you react to these problems. To learn more check out IDEA 51, *The Poseidon adventure*.

Try another idea...

Create a questionnaire to gauge customers' opinion of your selection of stock. As this is probably the showpiece of the business, it's a good place to start. Your questions should not focus on the aesthetics such as the quality of your racking or shop fitting (although one question of this type is fine). Most questions should be focused on the selection or ability to find the products they require, quickly and easily. Include space for customers to include their own comments and leave them with the question: 'If I could change one thing about this business it would be...'

The answers will be varied and strange, but depending on the size of your cross-section you will probably end up with over ten alterations that need to be made to the layout of the shop or warehouse. These answers are coming straight from your clients. Their reactions are real, if sometimes odd, and they will help give you an insight into who users are and why.

How did it go?

Q The sales manager doesn't want to send a questionnaire to customers without including some sort of promotion. He says it is a lost opportunity. Is this the right attitude?

A *Every business is different and it may be that you have to combine the two, but, adding a sales promotion, unless it is particularly attractive, is not going to help you get (honest) responses to the questionnaire – it will probably just confuse the message. Better to incentivise those who respond with either a specific promotion or a free gift.*

Q All of our responses were very encouraging and not at all negative – does this mean we have the perfect business?

A *Unlikely, it just means your questions were loaded to receive positive responses or your sample was badly chosen. Have someone else create the questions and make sure you select a cross-section of your customer base.*

HELP
WANTED

49

Time for reflection

Launching a business is hard work and can be all-consuming. However, we do have to take stock every once in a while and monitor how we are getting on.

Just as you would to cross a busy road, in business you should stop, look and listen every now and again to put it all into perspective.

Business is constantly changing. With technology becoming ever smarter and smaller, the digital age is doing a lot more for us than making our music collections portable. We should see technology as our friend and use it to help us in more ways than writing fancy letters. Assessing your own progress can be as scientific as you like, but there's no point in spending time and effort on the exercise if you are not reacting to the results. Just as the business plan you are writing will alter over the coming years, so should your projections. Once you begin trading you should capture the actual results and match your income and expenditure against your projections. If your projections are wildly high or far too low, you need to work on them again. Outperforming or underachieving is not telling you anything other than the projections were wrong. Use spreadsheets as much as possible to both capture and present the data.

Here's an idea for you...

When assessing your progress, be sure to acknowledge your successes as well as your failures. Reward yourself and your team every so often for making the business work – throw a party!

Although you will have annual targets in terms of turnover and expenditure, it is very useful to break the year into quarters and sometimes even individual months or weeks. Even if the benefits are still to show through as savings, are you and your staff becoming more efficient in the basics? What is your performance in answering queries by telephone and email and increasing the number of clients visiting your office or customers entering your premises? Have your staff attended the training courses you thought would be beneficial? Have any problems been dealt with, or are you constantly fire-fighting? Take a long, honest look at your business. Fixing problems will improve the long-term financial well-being of the organisation.

You can learn a lot from your competitors, but this does not mean that by copying them to the letter you will become as successful as they are. They may have had first-mover advantage and now have a loyal customer base. They may have had four times more seed capital to get their idea off the ground. The market may have been different a few years ago, so the exact same tactics will simply not work now.

Many retail outlets selling similar products will look pretty similar to consumers, except for a different colour pattern and branding. There's a good reason for this: the pattern works. You can launch a completely unique business without having to be wholly original all of the time. Why go through a long and expensive learning process when other companies have spent the money researching consumer preference and trends? Assess what is going on in the market around you and adapt.

Have a third-party professional assess what you have achieved thus far. It could be a formal review or just a quiet chat over lunch, but it will not be a wasted experience. After about six months of operations it would be well worth buttering up your accountant or solicitor and giving them an update of where you are. If you involved these people in the formation of the business and talked through the business plan with them, then they will be more than familiar with the background. How do they feel about the progress you are making? Do bear in mind that they will only be able to react to the information that you provide – the more honest your account of operations, the more informed and accurate their reply.

Try another idea...

For more about parties and in particular the all-important launch party that is probably going to happen in the none-too-distant future, check out IDEA 52, *Ladies in white bikinis.*

Defining idea...

'Reflect on your present blessings, of which every man has many; not on your past misfortunes, of which all men have some.'
CHARLES DICKENS

How did it go?

Q How should we treat our performance figures at monthly and quarterly meetings?

A *Prepare the figures well in advance and circulate them, highlighting any problem areas. Tell everyone that you expect them to be read before the meeting. This means that you can discuss the implications of your performance in much more practical terms at the meeting. If you have performed well unexpectedly, it is important to find out why, and to see if you can build upon the success.*

Q We are still behind target in terms of sales. Isn't a party a little extravagant?

A *There will be things you need to do to improve sales, but having a team that is motivated and content will make that task all the easier. This isn't about rewarding failure; it's about morale building.*

Q A party is beyond our budget, but I would like to reward effort and hard work. Is there anything else that I could do?

A *If you haven't done so already, it is always worth adding a competitive edge to the workplace. Providing the best salesperson with a bonus, or extra holiday, or some other tangible benefit will get the team working hard, for you.*

50

Elvis has left the building

When you first launch a business it may be your intention to work in it forever. It is best, however, to plan for potential exit routes right from the beginning.

Rather than racking up as much personal and business debt as possible and then flying off to Rio, you'll do much better to find legitimate ways to sell on your business.

It is not uncommon to launch a business with the sole intention of building it up to a certain level and then selling it on. A lot of money can be made this way if your offering is unique, popular and somehow taps into the Zeitgeist. Examples from the internet industry include Hotmail being bought by Microsoft to consolidate their position as the most popular free email provider and AOL merging with Time Warner to become one of the world's largest information/content providers.

If this is your intention, the focus of the business must be to grow really fast to let potential buyers know that you are in the market as a serious competitor and therefore a threat. They may try to buy you. It is not amoral to sell your business on, just make sure that the price is right when you come to sell.

Here's an idea for you...

List at least five organisations or individuals who could potentially be interested in acquiring your business. Once you have identified the parties, list what reason/s they would have for wanting to buy or merge with your company. Use this exercise as the first draft of your exit strategy within your business plan.

When you are compiling your business plan, be sure to list all potential buyers of your business. You don't need to approach these businesses to find out what they think of your proposal, just list a reason why they might be interested and explain what they would gain from buying/merging with your business.

People with lots of money usually spend lots of money and it is not uncommon for an individual who is interested in owning a business to buy one rather than start one. They may want to avoid the difficult part of setting the thing up and taking all of the initial risk; they can just simply write a big fat cheque for your trouble. More often than not, this is a win–win situation for both parties. You will, hopefully, get a good price for all those early mornings and late nights and your buyer walks into a functioning business with a stable infrastructure and a team of hard-working staff.

Defining idea...

'The leader has to be practical and a realist, yet must talk the language of the visionary and the idealist.'

ERIC HOFFER, American philosopher

In certain cases, especially when a third party wholly funds a business, it could be that there is a finite, pre-determined date when the company will finish. Project-based companies are no less important and no different to run than businesses that plan to stay around forever, but it is even more important that an exit strategy is clarified right from the beginning. This is so that all those involved are quite clear about what will happen in two, five or ten years time, especially with regard to the companies' assets, staff and, if applicable, debt. Drawing up a list of rules or directives now will save a lot of anguish in the years to come.

Try another idea...

To prepare your business for a potential sale you have to make the proposition as attractive as possible to all of your potential buyers. To learn more, check out IDEA 42, *Surrounded by winners.*

How did it go?

Q I am planning a home-based business through which I will provide management consultancy to struggling firms. I cannot really imagine other companies wanting to buy me out. Surely an exit strategy does not apply?

A While they might not want to buy the shed at the bottom of your garden from where you currently operate, a lot of rival firms may be very interested in your client list and teaching material. Never say never; someone, somewhere will be interested in buying your hard work from you.

Q I am concerned that the companies that I list within the exit strategy will not be operating by the time I am ready to sell. Won't this make my business plan dated if they go out of business themselves?

A *An exit strategy, much like the rest of the business plan, is flexible and can be modified and altered constantly. As long as you revisit each aspect of the plan at least once a year, it will never look dated.*

Q When is the best time to sell?

A *When your industry is booming and everyone is very optimistic about the future. You will get the best price at this time!*

Q When is the worst time to sell?

A *When your industry is in the dumps – or worse yet, when you are in trouble and everyone knows it. That's when the sharks move in to get the best bargain they can. Sell a business when everything is rosy – during the bad times, it's best just to manage it for survival.*

51

The Poseidon adventure

No matter how well crafted your plan, things can and often do go wrong; good business acumen is judged partly on how you minimise your risk but also on how well you deal with setbacks.

Despite the best will in the world and your best efforts, orders sometimes aren't what they should be. The question is, will you run or will you fight?

Quiet weeks quickly turn into quiet months and inevitably you have a lot more money going out than is coming in. There really is no point just hoping that things are going to turn out for the best and everything will sort itself out. It won't, not without a level of interaction from you. Keeping accurate records of your accounts is a minimum requirement for any business, but the trick is to actually read the data, try to make sense of the figures and look for tell-tale patterns. If you notice a downward spiral beginning to form, then react to it immediately rather than letting it get any worse. There are a number of options open to you if your cash flow is looking a tad negative:

Here's an idea for you...

If there is any way of ring-fencing funds for a 'rainy day', then do it. The funds do not have to sit in a separate account, nor is it a huge problem if you dip into the money occasionally to pay off invoices. Making this happen simply means negotiating hard on every deal and trying to cut costs wherever you can. If you can bring your expenditure down by 10% you'll have that much more room for manoeuvre.

Overdraft – Increasing your overdraft will be at your bank's discretion and may require personal guarantees from you that will mean you paying the debt off personally if the business cannot afford it. Assuming you can get the limit raised, this is probably the easiest way to cover the shortfall and can be the fastest way from realising there is a problem to being able to deal with it.

Loan – Borrowing additional funds when things seem to be getting bad can be a scary prospect, but it can also be the lifeline you need to ride out the storm and turn the business around. Whether you will be able to raise the money will depend on the amount that you have borrowed already, your likely ability to repay it and the amount required. A loan will mean additional monthly payments, which need to be accounted for, but it will also mean that creditors are kept happy and you have time to react to the situation.

Streamlining – Not a pleasant route at all, but one that must be considered. 'Streamlining' is a euphemism for letting staff go. There is often a short-term cost associated with making staff redundant – both financially and in terms of increased workload for others. In the long term, though, you will be saving significant amounts of money and it could be enough to fix your cash flow.

Selling off assets – Depending on what you have and how much of it is essential, you will soon decide whether this is a viable option. Although you will receive only about 30% of the original value of the items, it is probably the most painless of all the routes to regaining positive cash flow – and it's a lot easier to sell a couple of computers and desks than it is to let a member of staff go.

A number of sudden surprises and setbacks can be avoided if you fully appreciate the risks associated before you launch the business. To learn more, check out IDEA 47, *World domination.*

Try another idea...

Losing an important member of staff is a real blow to any business, no matter how big or small, but when you are a fledgling business the pain is all the more acute. There are numerous reasons why a staff member will want to leave and there is very little that you can do to stop the process. The most important thing is to always bear in mind that nothing is set in stone and no matter how well you get on with your staff, outside influences such as family, illness, rising house prices and, not least, better offers from elsewhere mean that on any day a staff member might resign from their position. Although you should not stay awake worrying about it, don't ignore it. No one is indispensable and therefore, whomever you deal with, in whatever capacity, from other companies or in your everyday life, they should always be assessed (privately, in your head!) as to his or her suitability within your business – one day you might just need to call upon them.

'We are continually faced with a series of great opportunities brilliantly disguised as insoluble problems.'
JOHN W. GARDNER, US politician

Defining idea...

How did it go?

Q We're not having much joy in bringing our suppliers' costs down – it's proving very hard to save any money. What are we doing wrong?

A *Your stock suppliers may not be willing to alter their margins at this stage, but if you budgeted X for a computer in the business plan and you can buy the same specification from a different manufacturer for 10% less, you will be well on your way to reducing costs.*

Q We have been unable to raise additional funds from the bank. Is there anything else we can do?

A *If you are absolutely confident that an injection of cash will see you through, and things are much more likely to get better after this dip, you can always raise the money privately through a personal bank loan or through borrowing from an affluent aunt, but only if you're sure…*

Q Our financial director says that we should not give any more credit to our best customer, even though he is ordering more each week. What is going on?

A *Your FD may be worried that your customer will suddenly stop paying the bills and you'll be left with a big loss. It is a very old trick to build up credit from suppliers and then go broke or take an age to pay. The way to manage it is to give each customer a credit limit and go through a formal process to increase it. A customer that increases their order by, say, a factor of ten over a short period can be very dangerous if you are financing their purchases.*

52

Ladies in white bikinis

So it has finally arrived: today is the day that you are officially operational and open for business. Have a wonderful party to celebrate, but remember to use the opportunity for more PR.

Do let your hair down and have some fun, but not so much that you are found in the corner unconscious with your eyebrows shaved off!

After all that planning, writing, thinking, worrying and every other emotion that goes into starting a business, it's launch day. For retail businesses, you are hoping to be swamped by calls or customers keen to spend their cash on your products. For commercial businesses, you are looking for orders being placed or meetings to take place that will lead to revenue generation. No matter what the business, today is the first day when real money will be changing hands and, hopefully, you will meet, if not exceed, projections.

Here's an idea for you...

Never shy away from a bit of PR; you could state on the invitation that each attendee is automatically entered into a draw to win products or services. Far be it for me to suggest in any way that the draw should be rigged, but wouldn't it be handy if the most influential business writer at a leading national were to win the first prize?

There is nothing that can be done now to improve the business plan (at least for today), no more adverts can be placed and no more staff can be called upon should you need them – you are launching with your opening gambit and it should pay off. For this one day only, try to relax and enjoy the experience. When it is closing time, it will be time to put the feet up, count your takings and open a bottle or two of bubbly.

Having a launch party serves a number of purposes. It is a reward to yourself, your staff and your family and friends for putting up with an obsessive taskmaster over the past few weeks. If day one proved to be slightly less successful than you had hoped, it is not the end of the world and will not be fixed this evening. Put it all to one side and enjoy the fruits of your labours. If you exceed your targets, great, but don't start altering your projections for the next three years just yet.

A launch party is a great way to get your business into the media once more, at a really significant time. By inviting journalists, presenters and researchers from the media, you stand a good chance of receiving a great story or feature, especially if there is a fair bit of booze on offer. For many businesses the launch party is the first time that members of the public or suppliers and investors have had an opportunity to see inside the shop or office. It completes the picture in many respects and cements the impression that you are here to stay. Do use the opportunity of a launch party to celebrate, but also use it as a way of promoting the business shamelessly.

Create the guest list for the launch party well in advance of the planned date. Once the date is set in stone (and there really isn't anything worse than this date slipping), create invitations and send them out. It is sometimes a good idea to 'soft-launch' the business for a week and then host the launch party at the end of your first week to allow for delays, but this all depends on the individual business.

Try another idea...

Hopefully, sometime in the future what started off as an idea and became a business plan will eventually become a hugely successful operation. There will come a point when you the business owner wants or needs to move on. There are a number of options open to you. To learn more, check out IDEA 50, *Elvis has left the building*.

Suddenly it is all very real and it can be a very nervous time. Don't lose sight of your objectives; if your planning is sound, you have the best people in the right jobs and everything is working the way it should, you are on your way to starting a successful business. Good luck with it all and enjoy the ride.

Defining idea...

'The public is wonderfully tolerant. It forgives everything except genius.'
OSCAR WILDE

How did it go?

Q Our business is very small and will operate from the spare room of my house. I hardly think this is a suitable location for a big party but I can't really afford to hire a venue. What can I do?

A *There are so many chains of restaurants, bars and hotels all fighting for custom that you can find venues that do not charge for room hire if you can give an indication of numbers. Some venues I have used in the past even put a small (tiny, actually) tab behind the bar and provided a few nibbles free of charge. Seek and ye shall find. Check it's not a strip joint, though!*

Q I would like to have a full colour invitation printed, but it seems like a waste of money. How can I create a good impression without spending a fortune?

A *There are excellent cheap colour printers available now; you can produce full colour invitations on your PC using software such as Photoshop, and print them out on card. It's well worth the effort if you can find someone to design it well.*

The end...

Or is it a new beginning? We hope that you've been inspired to get your new business really moving. You should be able to plan it so brilliantly that when potential investors see your proposal they'll be knocked out by the prospects of untold wealth. You know how to kick the competition into touch and the bank manager has already invited you for lunch. Let us know if that's the case. We'd like to be amazed and impressed too.

If there was an idea that you struggled to understand, tell us about that too. Tell us how you got on generally. What did it for you – what helped you to turn what everyone thought was just a pipe dream into reality? Maybe you've got some tips of your own that you want to share. If you liked this book you may find we have more brilliant ideas for other areas that could help change your life for the better.

You'll find the Infinite Ideas crew waiting for you online at www.infideas.com.

Or if you prefer to write, then send your letters to:
Smarter Business Start-ups
The Infinite Ideas Company Ltd
Belsyre Court, 57 Woodstock Road, Oxford OX2 6HJ, United Kingdom

We want to know what you think, because we're all working on making our lives better too. Give us your feedback and you could win a copy of another 52 *Brilliant Ideas* book of your choice. Or maybe get a crack at writing your own.

Good luck. Be brilliant.

Offer one

CASH IN YOUR IDEAS

We hope you enjoy this book. We hope it inspires, amuses, educates and entertains you. But we don't assume that you're a novice, or that this is the first book that you've bought on the subject. You've got ideas of your own. Maybe our author has missed an idea that you use successfully. If so, why not send it to info@infideas.com, and if we like it we'll post it on our bulletin board. Better still, if your idea makes it into print we'll send you £50 and you'll be fully credited so that everyone knows you've had another Brilliant Idea.

Offer two

HOW COULD YOU REFUSE?

Amazing discounts on bulk quantities of Infinite Ideas books are available to corporations, professional associations and other organizations.

For details call us on:
+44 (0)1865 292045
fax: +44 (0)1865 292001
or e-mail: info@infideas.com

Where it's at...

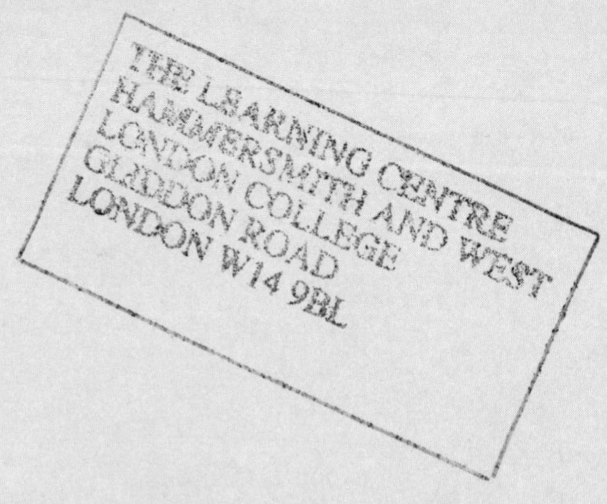

Even more brilliant ideas...

Unleash your creativity

Rob Bevan & Tim Wright

"Isn't being creative something you're born with, like blonde hair or blue eyes? Can we really show you how to be a creative genius?"

"Well, in our experience most people are amazed to discover just how creative they can be. So how do you find the real, inspired, creative YOU? It's all about mindset actually. You just need to cut through the blinkered thinking that everyday life perpetuates. We've seen people transform themselves simply by being in the right environment, with the right people and learning a few simple techniques. Unleash your creativity will teach you how to make those ideas explode!"
– **Rob Bevan and Tim Wright**

Available from all good bookshops and online at www.amazon.co.uk

---

Transform your life

Penny Ferguson

"At the age of 49 I was walking in the woods and taking stock of my life so far. It wasn't a pleasant experience. I'd been abandoned by my mother when I was four months old. I'd been teased and bullied at school and had been physically and mentally wrecked by not one, not two, but three abusive marriages. To top it all off I was broke. With such low self-esteem, I knew I was rubbish at everything."

"There and then I resolved that I just wasn't going to continue to waste the rest of my life. I knew that I had to change my life, and that meant changing me. And I've succeeded. I'm 61 now, successful and happy, and have helped thousands of people to do the same. Transform your life *tells you how. Enjoy life! And become the person you really want to be!"* – **Penny Ferguson**

Web sites that work

Jon Smith

"Web site design. All a bit mysterious and scary isn't it? As if only a few chosen individuals have been ordained into some techno brotherhood that speaks and writes in a different language, punctuated by Java scripts, Dreamweavers, CSSs and HTML code."

"You don't have to have a BSc in Nerdiness or know what Bill Gates had for breakfast to get to grips with web design. Why stick to the tired and out-of-date site you currently have? Ordinary non-techy folk just like you can have a web site that looks great, but more importantly, does exactly what you want it to do without you having to learn a programming language. Let me show you how. I'll help you to re-energise your web site so that it can achieve exactly what you want it to." **– Jon Smith**

High-impact CVs

John Middleton

"Your CV should be the single most powerful weapon in your job-hunting armoury. It should hit a potential employer's desk and scream "give me that job...!" Yet I must have looked at over 25,000 CVs in my time in various HR and personnel roles and most of them screamed "bin me immediately...!" instead."

"The rest were either so dull that they sent me into a coma or so full of the almost godlike qualities of the applicant that I felt like returning them with a post-it note saying "verily we are not worthy..."

"So just think... If you hit all the right buttons with a potential employer, you can secure that sought-after job and at the same time help reduce the number of work days lost to comas annually!" – **John Middleton**